Raising
Sebastien

Raising Sebastien

Realising the Potential of Your Autistic Child

by **Choo Kah Ying**

 **Marshall Cavendish** Editions

Published by Marshall Cavendish Editions
An imprint of Marshall Cavendish International
1 New Industrial Road, Singapore 536196

Other Marshall Cavendish Offices:
Marshall Cavendish Ltd. 119 Wardour Street, London W1F 0UW, UK • Marshall Cavendish Corporation. 99 White Plains Road, Tarrytown NY 10591-9001, USA • Marshall Cavendish International (Thailand) Co Ltd. 253 Asoke, 12th Flr, Sukhumvit 21 Road, Klongtoey Nua, Wattana, Bangkok 10110, Thailand • Marshall Cavendish (Malaysia) Sdn Bhd, Times Subang, Lot 46, Subang Hi-Tech Industrial Park, Batu Tiga, 40000 Shah Alam, Selangor Darul Ehsan, Malaysia

Marshall Cavendish is a trademark of Times Publishing Limited

National Library Board Singapore Cataloguing in Publication Data

Choo, Kah Ying.
Raising Sebastien : realising the potential of your autistic child / Choo Kah Ying. – Singapore Marshall Cavendish Editions, c2006.
p. cm.
ISBN-13 : 978-981-261-320-2
ISBN-10 : 981-261-320-X

1. Autistic children. 2. Autistic children – Education. 3. Autism in children 4. Child rearing.
I. Title.

HQ773.5
649.154 -- dc22   SLS2006029801

Printed in Singapore by Times Graphics Pte Ltd

To SEBASTIEN, my fellow traveller, on this extraordinary journey of unconditional love and perseverance.

CONTENTS

PROLOGUE

It was a magical twilight hour, not too long after the sun had set, but the encroaching darkness had already chased away the remainder of the beachgoers and the sunset gazers. At that time of the day, you could barely make out the drifting boundary where the ocean and the beach meet. The beach had already lost its sunshiny allure that drew many to the sand during the day.

Only two figures remained—two barely discernible silhouettes in the dying light from the perspective of someone standing on the Santa Monica Pier in Los Angeles, California. From his point of view, this stranger might have been able to make out the contours of a woman's body with long flowing hair whipping around in the evening breeze. She was walking hand-in-hand with a toddler near the water. Together, they constituted an odd couple lingering on the beach beyond the typical hours for mothers and young children. Lingering even though the sun had disappeared and taken with it traces of its warmth.

That odd couple was my son and me in the autumn of 1997, mere months before our private idyllic days would be scattered into the wind and all hell would break loose. Neither of us could have seen it coming as we paced along the beach in the amazing quiet. Both of us were captivated by the perfect silence of this magical hour.

Only the unpredictable invasion of the startlingly cold sensation of the seawater on our feet jolted our senses. Ignoring the darkness, the cold clammy feel of my jeans against my legs and the incessant drone of my inner voice telling me that we should get back, we continued to linger at the beach. Sebastien, only 13 months old, seemingly oblivious of the cold, was stumbling 'carefreely' on the uneven surface of the wet sand. Caught up in a moment like this when all was peaceful and quiet, fears of what might be lurking beyond the darkness, beyond the magical hour, somehow eluded us.

Little did we know that in just three months, Sebastien would be diagnosed with autistic affect—the precursor to autism.

*****

Whether you like it or not, raising an autistic child will thrust you into uncharted territory. Autism is a baffling condition whose cause has yet to be determined, though speculations abound. Autistic individuals, depending on their functioning levels in different areas, occupy a vast spectrum that stretches from 'mild' to 'severe'. Because of their unique combinations of strengths and deficits, you will not find one autistic individual who is similar to another. Thus, it is difficult to replicate approaches found to be effective for one autistic child for another and expect similar successes.

Nonetheless, for the sake of readers who are unfamiliar with autism, I would still like to provide my perspective of autism, which captures its unique aspects, regardless of the diverse functioning levels of the autistic individuals. Based on my encounters and interactions, I see that all autistic people are characterised by an inability to interpret social cues and norms that shape human behaviour and practices. As a consequence, they are unable to comprehend and apprehend the human experience that is grasped intuitively by typical people without any conscious effort.

Because of their lack of a 'social' frame of reference to help them understand mainstream society, autistic people often rely on routines and fixations to enable them to impose order and predictability on what they view as an exceedingly incomprehensible human world. For those who have heightened sensory perceptions to their environment, their routines and fixations can also exert a calming influence on their beings. Nonetheless, while these routines allow autistic people to maintain a measure of sanity and control, their systematic nature, their repetitiveness and rigidities can often prove to be maddening for typical human beings who are far less systematic.

The collision of the two worlds, as represented by the differences in the perceptions and experiences between autistic people and mainstream society, is what makes raising an autistic child such a challenging endeavour. Over the last few years, Sebastien and I are continually forced to step out of our respective comfort zones and cross the divide. Through these struggles, we forge a loving relationship that transcends these irreconcilable differences between autistic people and their typical counterparts.

This book documents our extraordinary journey.

INTRODUCTION

This book was originally conceived as a result of an interview that took place in 2004 with a researcher from the University of Wisconsin who was doing a follow-up research study on the coping challenges confronted by parents raising an autistic child. The previous interview had taken place four years ago. When I saw her e-mail requesting for a follow-up interview, I leapt at the opportunity to tell her about how far along the road I had travelled on my journey with Sebastien who was eight years old at the time of the second interview.

Attached to her e-mail was a research article that she had written based on her first set of interviews with the mothers of autistic children. Because the identities of the participants were concealed by pseudonyms, I struggled to determine which portions of the article referred to me and Sebastien. Although she had assumed that I would be able to recognise references to the two of us in the article, I felt truly estranged from the experiences of all the mothers depicted in the article. Although the experiences sounded familiar, they seemed to belong to a previous life—one of which I had once known, but no longer inhabited.

Essentially, I was no longer one of the mothers who lamented about the difficulties of raising an autistic child. I did not consider my responsibility of bringing up an autistic child to be a burden. It was a sentiment, a change in perspective within me that I tried hard to convey to this researcher during an interview that was supposed to have lasted for an hour, but stretched beyond three hours.

Two things struck me about the interview that day as I saw the tears glistening in this researcher's eyes while I talked about my relationship with my son, as well as my growing love and respect for him. I realised then that I had a story that was worth telling—a narrative to which no research article with all its academic requirements could do justice. I did not want my voice, my story and my child to be subsumed within an objective piece of research, blending with other voices within a thematic context constructed by the researcher. Essentially, we would be trapped in this scientific realm that could only partially capture a fragment of our reality and our identities.

Even more importantly, I do not believe that life with an autistic child is simply about coping. Casting our life in a negative light does not fully encompass its reality. At least it has not been for me in the last few years with my growing experience and understanding of my child and his baffling condition. Ultimately, I realise that if I want my story to be told, I will have to tell it my way.

My encounter with this researcher led to the writing of the series of essays that are found in the first major section of this book under 'Reflections'. This series of essays chart my observations of Sebastien from the early days of diagnosis to the most recent developments in his growth during the last five months. Although each of these essays have been fine-tuned and edited recently, I have chosen to insert the date of the original writing of the essay to highlight the evolution of my ever-changing perspectives on Sebastien and autism.

The second section, 'Practical Suggestions', came into being upon my return to Singapore in August 2005. Having lived in the United States (US) for the last 12 years, I was utterly unprepared for the lack of public assistance, along with affordable educational and therapeutic services, for families of children with autism in Singapore. Many of these services are provided free of charge by the public agencies in the US once the child is determined to be on the autistic spectrum. What was even more startling to me was the lack of empowerment of some parents in Singapore who are so desperate for any services that they are willing to put up with an inadequate quality of care and education provided to their children because of the dearth of real alternatives.

Because of my exposure to the educational and therapeutic services in the US and my long struggle to raise Sebastien, I realise that I possess tremendous knowledge, experience and the resilience to make a positive change in the autism community in Singapore. More specifically, I set out to empower parents to take control of the education and the raising of their children through parent training programmes.

'Practical Suggestions'—the training manual segment is the culmination of not only the knowledge I acquired from various books and professionals (both good and bad) encountered in the US, but also the product of many triumphs and many more heartbreaks. Through my struggles by trial and error to help my son to make eye contact, talk, read, write and interact with others, I have become empowered through my successes and persistence in dealing with some of his most distressing issues such as aggression.

Even though I was living in a country full of professionals and specialists in the field of autism, I discovered that I could often identify and resolve the problems encountered by my son long before those who were supposed to know better. Many a times, professionals will shrug their shoulders in frustration and declare that my child belongs to that one per cent that does not respond to their specific therapy. "He should be talking by now," was a declaration that I had heard time and time again.

Consequently, over the last four years, I began to take the lead in formulating and implementing interventions for my son and asking the professionals to work on my concerns with him in other settings. The decision to take charge of his learning when Sebastien turned five and still could not imitate speech, as well as my success in helping him to speak, read and write, would change my life forever.

It is important to point out that this book is not designed to replace services. It is rather meant to serve as a supplement to current therapeutic and educational services received by these autistic children. Essentially, parents will acquire practical ideas and strategies, which can be executed affordably to fill in the gaps in any of the services.

Moreover, in this section, I put forth what I believe to be a novel conception of education for children with autism—a holistic and integrated approach to education. This educational model goes against the prevailing conventional approach in special education that compartmentalises the task of working with an autistic child into highly specialised disciplines.

Specifically, there is a speech therapist who deals with the autistic child's lack of speech and/or communication difficulties; an occupational therapist who addresses the child's sensory difficulties; an educator who handles the child's academic learning; a physical therapist who deals with the gross motor challenges of the child; and so on and so forth.

While these different specialists offer invaluable insights into the treatment of an autistic child, they only focus on their own specialised areas without taking into consideration the whole child. As a result, an autistic child can often be reduced into a series of discrete deficits as though one has no connection with the other. Therefore, parents play a vital role of piecing their child together and adopting a holistic and integrated perspective of their child. At the end of the day, parents are the only ones who are aware of all the treatments undergone by their children and their outcomes. They also bear witness to their children's reactions and behaviours in a variety of settings, away from the educational and therapeutic environments.

Finally, I want to emphasise that this book is not an end-product. It is rather an evolving work-in-progress as I continue to trudge along on this challenging journey. Through my work with my son and others in my parent training and consultation programmes, I am continuing to hone my knowledge and understanding of autistic children and autism in general. I hope that my constant striving to love and raise Sebastien with the attention and care he deserves will continue to offer me precious insights and enhance my endeavours to help others.

Now, I would like to extend an invitation to you to walk with me on this uncharted and life-transforming journey.

Section One
REFLECTIONS

Chapter One
Surviving the Early Years

My Journey

I am the proud mother of Sebastien—my nine-year-old autistic son. It has taken years of learning how to teach him to acquire basic skills that most people take for granted and surviving the accompanying heartbreaks to make this statement with my chin held up high.

My statement should not be misinterpreted to mean that Sebastien displays any awe-inspiring talents or abilities typically associated with high-functioning autistic people or autistic savants. In fact, in that regard, he is rather ordinary. To place him on the wide autistic spectrum ranging from mild to severe autism, I would say that Sebastien is a moderately autistic child with severe language delays.

Diagnosed at the age of 18 months with autistic affect, Sebastien was regarded as a textbook case of autism with his sudden, but complete, loss of facial affect (expressions), absence of any types of sounds, failure to point and the lack of eye contact. His inability to produce any speech, in spite of intensive speech therapy for more than three years and his obvious intelligence, led me to recognise the severity of his language delays. Through a modified form of the Applied Behavioural Analysis (ABA) approach, I, along with a trainee behaviourist, was finally able to teach Sebastien how to imitate phonetic sounds. By then, he was already five years old.

Today, he is a child who reads and writes far better than he speaks. Through careful management and alternative healing therapies, Sebastien's aggression seems to have disappeared completely. Even as he continues to struggle with his speech and experiences difficulties in communicating with others, Sebastien has learned to compensate for them by using strong non-verbal communication skills that demonstrate a sophisticated understanding of how typical people relate to one another.

Although his accomplishments to date are commendable and gratifying to me, it is the journey that he has travelled that makes him an extraordinary child in my eyes. As his mother, I have truly seen him travel along the road less travelled from the unresponsive and withdrawn child of the past to become an animated, curious and passionate lover of life. Being the primary witness of his efforts, I can tell you that it has not been an easy road.

Let me take you back to the beginning.

God Rage
(Los Angeles, March 2004)

For most parents of children with autism, the worst possible day is the day that they receive the diagnosis of autism for the first time. I was certainly not so calm and collected three months after my idyllic walk on that beach when a doctor stared at my son with her guarded demeanour.

From her expression, one would not know that she was gazing at an 18-month-old toddler who was bewildered by the stacks of unfamiliar cubes placed in front him. Rather, she looked at him as though he were a caged lion prowling restlessly in its prison, waiting for the opportunity to lash out at her should she let down her guard for a second.

A moment later, she gestured at me to move back to give him space. Feeling utterly confused by her behaviour, I was raging in my head: "What is the big deal about these dumb cubes? So what if he does not want to stack them? Even I don't want to stack them!" At the same time, I felt my face and my body growing hot from the sheer effort of trying to get Sebastien to adhere to this doctor's instructions.

Upon hindsight, I often wondered if the doctor was actually bracing for the appropriate moment to tell me. Perhaps, inwardly, she was dreading the prospect of being the messenger breaking the bad news, of being the one to tell me that my life was about to turn upside down. A woman in her fifties, she must have known that, in just a brief moment, she would have to dash away a mother's aspirations for her child and his future—however vague and amorphous they might have been when he was only an 18-month-old toddler.

"As I suspected, he has an autistic affect, the precursor to autism. Since he is so young, I cannot make a definite diagnosis. But at the UCLA clinic where I work with many autistic children, I can see that your son possesses many of the classic characteristics..." At some point, I lost track of her exact words as she informed me about the services and assistance which were available and gave me contact information.

Only the words *Rain Man* pounded in my head. My son and his future were encapsulated in the image of the Dustin Hoffman character in a film that I barely remembered. All I could recall were the man's dependence on others in adulthood; the awkwardness of his mannerisms; the flatness of his facial expression; and the monotony of his voice, stripped of life and vitality. It was hard to imagine my son growing up to be like *Rain Man*.

I don't remember how I made it home that day. All I can remember is pulling out the Diagnostic and Statistical Manual of Mental Disorders (DSM-IV) to look up the scientific catalogue of the symptoms under 'autism'. In that blinding instant, all of Sebastien's erratic behaviours during the last three months made a lot of sense. Once he turned 15 months old, he began to lose interest in his toys and his surroundings. For three months, he had gazed disinterestedly at toys and refused to acknowledge the existence of people around him. His sole interest lay in watching the tempestuous ocean crash against the wooden planks that held up the Santa Monica Pier.

By that time, any trace of human emotion or expression had disappeared, only to be replaced by an eerie explosion of giggles that would erupt out of the blue, without any apparent cause. His animation, his playfulness and his zeal for life, which blazed from his eyes, were only evident in my snapshots of him when he was younger. It was as though a dark cloud had moved across the sun and taken away its warmth and brightness.

We were virtually leading a cave-like existence as Sebastien screamed and cried every time I spoke to neighbours and tried to visit others even for a moment. Craving the security and predictability of each day, he dictated how he wanted us to walk to the pier—what turns to take at which streets—by throwing temper tantrums.

Still, I had dismissed these behaviours as a phase—hellish, but temporary. As a new mother, I was proud that I had survived the difficult months of his infancy. From the day he was born, Sebastien had posed a formidable challenge. Apart from the first day of his life in which he slept soundly throughout the day, he refused to sleep for too long. It was a miracle if he slept for more than three hours at a stretch during the night. Most of the time, he woke up every hour to guzzle on his bottle before falling back to sleep. In spite of his intermittent sleep during the night, he was unwilling to take naps during the day, his mind propelling his body forward and onward like a cruel master that would not offer any respite, until he grew cranky and miserable. This crankiness would persist for two days before he finally collapsed into a state of rest. To top it all off, he was a cranky infant who was not easily appeased by food, drink or human comfort.

With the heavy manual weighing heavily on my lap, I remember staring in horror at this toddler who had stopped smiling for months and making any types of sounds. My son had turned into an alien child with whom I could not identify. It was not just a phase, a temporary period. The permanence of his condition overwhelmed me that evening as I vented all my anguish, sadness and fury at God.

As I stood at the sink washing dishes, doing anything just to stop looking at Sebastien and wishing for this nightmare to end, I ranted and raged at God. What kind of God would inflict such an act of injustice on a young child, destroying his future and sealing his fate when his life had barely begun? Once upon a time, I had promised myself that my son would have a better life than I would. On that evening, I felt that God had let me down because I could no longer live up to that promise.

Even in this dark moment, however, I was blessed by an enlightening conversation with a close friend who resided in San Diego. As I poured forth my feelings about the 'alien' Sebastien, he set me on the right path by making this simple statement: "You know Sebastien is still the same child, before and after the doctor's visit." The simplicity of my friend's statement woke me up from my hysteria and frenzy so that I could properly grieve the loss of my son on the toughest day in the life of any parent with a child with special needs. Nonetheless, it would take another six months before I was able to gaze at my son with complete love and acceptance of his fate, as he slept serenely. So serenely that a stranger looking down at this child would not think that anything was amiss, that this child and his mother had just gone through another difficult day of tantrums and misery. I would not know this at the time, but these poignant moments of tranquility as I watched Sebastien sink into a deep slumber and wept profusely would prove to be part and parcel of my journey towards my acceptance of Sebastien as an autistic child.

Only with this acceptance was I freed from the paralysis of indecision—straddling between the two worlds of hope and reality. The next morning, I brought Sebastien to one of my favourite professors in college in Los Angeles, who was a psychiatrist, an artist and an incredibly kind-hearted woman.

In her office, she quietly observed Sebastien playing with a framed painting on the wall by swinging it from side to side. After 15 minutes, she remarked that he had not once made eye contact with her. Meeting her compassionate gaze, I realised then that I was ready for this news because it did not devastate me. As we sat in the room and the setting sun shot its dying rays into the studio-like room, she showed me a photocopy of the autistic spectrum and asked me where I would place Sebastien on the spectrum based on his symptoms. Studying the paper closely, I situated Sebastien on the moderate portion of the spectrum with a severe speech delay.

Even though the memories of that day have begun to grow hazy in my mind, I will never forget that moment when I stepped out into the cool evening breeze of June. Instead of being overwhelmed by despair by the confirmation of his condition, I experienced an uplifting feeling of relief. The struggle was over. My son has autism. In that moment, I gave myself permission to embrace Sebastien with complete and unconditional love by bidding farewell to the son I had hoped against all odds would somehow return to me.

That was only the beginning, however. Back then, I did not have an inkling of how challenging my life with Sebastien would be in the subsequent years. Had I known how hard it would be, I do not think I would have had that moment of clarity and relief. I certainly did not know that in the two years after his diagnosis, I would not be able to interact with my son who would do anything to avoid making eye contact with everyone, who resembled the hollow shell of a child who was only physically present, but whose mind seemed to occupy an entirely different plane of existence in actuality. Where he was back then, I would never know.

Yet even the darkness of those days was dissipated by the sheer radiance of the 'wonder moments'.

The Wonder Moments
(Los Angeles, March 2004)

One of the primary preoccupations of parents and practitioners in the pediatric field is the milestones reached by children. In the early years, whether and when the children reach pre-designated milestones is an indicator of whether they are experiencing any developmental delay that is a cause for alarm for the parents.

Once he mastered walking at around 11 ½ months of age, Sebastien simply veered off the path trodden by many of his typical peers. At that point, pediatricians started highlighting the many milestones that he had not reached.

He did not point. He did not make any sounds, let alone words, or even sentences by the age of two. If you were to fill in a development assessment form for him, it would be more a catalogue of what he was not able to do, instead of what he was able to do for his age level.

In spite of his developmental disorder, however, I have continued to celebrate Sebastien's milestones—the ones that differ radically from those of people in mainstream society. His are the milestones that are reserved for those who are often relegated to the periphery of society, such as individuals with special needs. As a parent of an autistic child, I have thus adopted a completely different perspective of milestones or achievements. My perspective is one that goes beneath the surface of the spectacular milestones treasured by mainstream society to acknowledge the tiny miracles in our lives, which may easily have gone unnoticed and unappreciated by most.

I have learnt to construct my own map of milestones, since there really is not one for autistic children and each autistic child is so different from another. In my own map of developmental milestones,

I include many events that are ignored by typical parents. I am not suggesting that these parents are poor parents because they take their children's typical development for granted. In their shoes, I, too, would have disregarded these events.

As a typical human being, I know that most of us are not programmed to linger on ordinary events that are accomplished with ease, that occur as expected on schedule. We glaze over these events, celebrate them maybe for the briefest of moments, before charging on to bigger and better things. After all, this is how humans have made their progress over the centuries, with our eyes aimed at the bright future, not by lingering on past accomplishments that have been attained.

When you live with an autistic child, however, you get to be really good at detecting these miracles—the unexpected gaze of recognition; the exchange of two-word conversations; and the first spontaneous utterance of 'I love you'. These are the moments when time stands still and your mind does a dance of euphoria that lifts you away from your surroundings. You tend to replay the moment again and again and savour its pleasure...before relinquishing it to memory, while allowing time to move on and your being to return to the reality of the everyday world. These moments are all the more precious because they can be easily missed. I am sure that in spite of my vigilance, I do miss quite a few of them.

For Sebastien, most of the developmental milestones (both the ones I included and those that are a part of the developmental milestones for a typical child) were not attained with ease. Moreover, the achievement of these milestones was often so long overdue that I almost doubted whether they would ever occur. Such that when they did occur, they were almost always unexpected. Their occurrence, as with an unexpected astrological event, would often leave me shell-shocked for a few seconds, as I process the new information in my state of shock.

The first couple of times when they happened, I felt the urge to move on quickly to the next milestone, knowing that Sebastien had so much more ground to cover, so much catching up to do. This urge reflected my failure to adapt to Sebastien's pace, until I was once again overwhelmed with frustration and anguish at his seeming lack of progress.

At some point, it dawned on me that I needed to stop battering myself against a brick wall that was not budging. Regardless of how hard I pushed Sebastien, that conventional milestone I was aiming for was receding further and further away. I had to admit that I had deluded myself into thinking that my child was able to follow the path of the developmental trajectory of a typical child. Then I would experience a great surge of sadness—the crushing wave of powerlessness that I had kept at bay as I invested all my effort and attention in my enthusiastic quest for the next milestone—and let go of my unrealistic expectations.

After going through the vicious cycles of hope, frustration and disillusionment, I have finally learned to embrace the fact that Sebastien and I are creating our own one-of-a-kind map of his developmental milestones. Eight years later, I have come to respond to his milestones in a way that does not send me spinning around in frenzy. Accepting that these events occur in between periods that vary in their lengths of time, I have adopted a more sane and pleasurable strategy to respond to them.

In the process, I have mastered the art of lingering, of stopping to smell the roses. I can savour the moment when it occurs and hold onto the euphoria of finally reaching that target that may have seemed unattainable only moments before. Because I have waited so long for these moments, when they do arrive, I feel the surrounding world recede from me as I dwell in my own mind, mentally hugging myself and patting Sebastien on his head, as I am immersed in mixed feelings that make me want to cry. An intermingling of triumph, relief, happiness and pride.

Yes, I feel a sense of pride towards Sebastien, in the same way that people offer the most thunderous applause to the last person who crosses the finishing line at the marathon. Except in our case, it is a celebration that takes place in complete solitude because no one else, not even Sebastien, can fully appreciate the significance of this event. In spite of the comparative insignificance of his achievement, I continue to marvel at watching him—a child who lacks the intuitive and spontaneous capacity to talk and thus socialise with others—making his painstaking steps on his path of growth and development.

Most of the time, I wonder how he keeps going, waking up every morning and raring to go out into a world where he has to struggle to do all the things that his peers do effortlessly. While the words pour out of their mouths, Sebastien grapples with the sheer effort of enunciating each syllable of each word to shape them into something barely intelligible and comprehensible.

Since his achievements often do not resemble the developmental milestones of typical children, I have come up with my own terminology. I have dubbed them the 'wonder moments' because these are the points of time that make your hard work worth its while. Now, without further ado, here are three of Sebastien's wonder moments.

First Sustained Eye Contact

Although I do not consider this to be one of the most spectacular wonder moments in our life, I will never forget it because it was the very first 'wonder moment'. More significantly, it served as a beacon of hope during my darkest hour.

Sebastien was about two years old at the time, six months after the initial diagnosis of his autistic affect. We had just entered the world of in-home therapy after he had tantrummed and cried his way out of an early intervention programme at the University of California, Los Angeles (UCLA). Twice a week, Sarah, a fun and talkative Jewish woman, lugged a big bag of preschool toys to our apartment and tried to engage Sebastien in play.

One of the first objectives was to get Sebastien to make eye contact—an amazingly difficult task for him that he repeatedly avoided. Regardless of what she did—sticking her face in his face or tempting him with an object of interest—he would weave his head up and down, back and forth, or from side to side, just to evade her gaze.

What was most difficult about those sessions was being forced to see Sebastien's deficits in painful clarity. Watching him from the sidelines, I could see the absence of expression in his face; the listlessness in his eyes; and his unwillingness to acknowledge Sarah's playful entreaties. Week after week she came, and week after week, I despaired that he would ever make any progress. Those were the darkest of days when my being was so deprived of any of the 'wonder moments' that would feed and sustain me in the subsequent years. I was a starving and hungry mother, waiting to pounce on anything for that sign of life.

And then, one day, it happened. During one of these sessions, when Sebastien had wandered away from the therapist and me towards the window, he suddenly turned around to stare at me. It was the longest sustained gaze he had given me since his symptoms started. Here was a child who had stopped looking into anyone's eyes. Taken completely by surprise, I could barely hold the gaze of his blazing eyes. They emitted so much power and life that I felt weak in their presence. But there it was—the first sign of life. Sebastien wanted me to know that he was alive and kicking, even though he might be hibernating in his world.

That 'wonder moment' represented by those blazing eyes would sustain me for the next two years, before I got to experience other 'wonder moments'. These early 'wonder moments' were like breadcrumbs that were barely enough to sustain anyone. In retrospect, however, I realise that the pitiful sustenance of these breadcrumbs trained me for the rigours of the journey ahead; taught me to tighten my belt; forced me to transcend the insatiable human desire for more; and compelled me to be grateful for each of the 'wonder moments'. Thus, I learnt to wait patiently, to be vigilant and alert to seize the next 'wonder moments'.

First Successful Imitation of Sounds
"He is so bright he should be talking by now."

This was a statement that I heard time and time again from Sebastien's school teacher, speech therapist, occupational therapist and behaviourist, when he turned three and then four. In spite of my attempts at being patient, I was really starting to despair at the prospect of him ever talking, reading and writing by the conventional means. The age of 'three' had been the magical signpost that I had hoped would mark the time when he would achieve many of his milestones such as talking and being toilet-trained. Looking back on his life, I realise that the magical age arrived when he was almost five years old.

One month shy of his fifth birthday, Sebastien's behaviourist and I finally achieved an incredible breakthrough. For the last nine months, the behaviourist and I had been trying in vain to get Sebastien to imitate phonetic sounds of the alphabet with the verbal command:

"Say 'B'. " Although we succeeded in getting Sebastien to imitate the sound 'b', by pointing a toy microphone at him, which emitted an echoing sound, he did not imitate any other sounds. Regardless of what we said, the moment we pointed the microphone at him, he would say 'b'. It took us months before we saw that the toy mike that was once an aid was now a hindrance to us.

In conformity with the practice of the behavioural approach of discrete trials, the behaviourist said that it was important to 'fade' out this prompt. So he issued the command, stuck the mike out at Sebastien and took it away the moment Sebastien opened his mouth. With the benefit of hindsight, I saw that we should simply have substituted a new object to stick at Sebastien with each new sound.

After one month of fading out this prompt, Sebastien finally understood what we wanted him to do one afternoon.
"Say 'B'. " "B."
"Say 'G'. " "G."
"Say 'M'. " "M."

After waiting for almost five years for this moment, I was honestly unprepared for its arrival and the momentousness of this event would take days to sink in. Over the next few days, I was caught up with getting Sebastien to repeat the alphabets, say 'mama' and 'Yuri'; and common one-syllable words. The behaviourist was amazed that Sebastien was able to repeat the alphabets within a week through repeated practice with me. My happiness dissipated, however, as it became apparent to me that Sebastien was simply imitating language without the ability to spontaneously generate them. Soon after, the behaviourist departed from our life and I took on the massive task of building on his language capacity.

Even though I did not appreciate the 'wonder moment' at the time (as much as I should have), I often replayed it in my head and quietly acknowledge the momentousness of this event during the subsequent years. In spite of the many discouraging days that would follow when Sebastien's budding speech was accompanied by early signs of aggression such as pinching, I still acknowledge this moment as a major breakthrough that finally ushered him into the world of language.

First Spontaneous Conversation

Two years after Sebastien imitated speech, he was able to speak in short sentences with prompting and made barely intelligible two-word requests for routine food items. You would not know how many times I had cooked instant 'noodles' for him when he was really requesting for 'soda'! That was how unintelligible he was. Still, it was better than no sounds at all. The fact that he, who had been so reluctant to speak because he saw no purpose in it, had finally grasped the significance of language as a means of communication constituted a huge leap in his development.

Nonetheless, I still could not help feeling frustrated that all the speech that ever came out of his mouth was either prompted by me, or referred to his favourite food or routines. In other words, our exchanges remained scripted and repetitive. I wondered how long I could sustain the effort of 'inputting' words into his mind, as though it were a tape recorder and having it played back to me. Ultimately, I was dismayed by the fact that Sebastien's emergence of language did not offer me a window into his mind. Apart from his requests for food items or the computer, I really did not know what he was thinking.

Until that day when we had our first spontaneous conversation in his favourite toy store called 'Puzzle Zoo' on the Santa Monica Promenade. He was seven years old. At the time of our visit, he had just begun to be interested in a relatively new 'Hot Wheels' display—a track that was shaped like a roller coaster—the reason underlying his interest in the toy car display.

On that day, however, no car was available at the 'Hot Wheels' display for him to play with. Knowing his attachment to routines and this display, I experienced a brief moment of panic. Searching for an alternative, I grabbed a toy train from a train set display and handed it over to him as a substitute: "No car, train." I made this offering calmly, though inside, I was trembling, uncertain how he, who always preferred the 'original' version of his experience, would react.

As my hand wavered, while he reflected for a moment, he plucked the train out of my hand. Then he placed it on the upside down portion of the track, looked up at me and said very clearly, "Roller coaster." Five-and-a-half years into the journey, I was savvy enough to grasp this 'wonder moment'—our first spontaneous conversation that deviated from the usual repertoire. For the briefest instant, I knew exactly what he was thinking. Just as significantly, he had demonstrated a capacity for imagination by transforming the train into the roller coaster and indicating his preference for the train over the car.

While Sebastien proceeded to play with his 'roller coaster', I launched myself into my 'wonder moment' space and time. Even though I was in a toy store, I felt as though I was in a world of my own, my mind replaying the words 'roller coaster' over and over again. For one precious minute, I gave myself a timeout to celebrate—my private celebration of reaching another wonder moment.

So as you can see, Sebastien's 'wonder moments' are completely different from those of his typical peers. In the eyes of most people, they may be dismissed as slim pickings that are hardly worth the effort. Even for me, these moments of triumph are often tinged with an inevitable sense of sadness. We have to fight so hard and so long for so little. Yet, when I take a step back to think outside the box of conventional society, I am able to acknowledge the significance of these achievements. I can see that it is not reaching the 'destination' that makes these wonder moments so special, but the hard-fought journey that get us there. Therein lies the wonder of these precious moments.

Setting the Bar Realistically High
(Los Angeles, March 2004)

As the mother of an autistic child, I have often been torn between these two opposing positions—pushing Sebastien to fit into mainstream society versus giving him the breathing room to engage in his strange mannerisms. For many parents of children with special needs, it is a dilemma they cope with not only on a daily basis, but also on a moment-to-moment basis, especially in the public space. How do you decide where to draw the line between tolerating certain types of behaviours and cracking down on them? How fair is it to expect your autistic child to behave like a typical child in certain settings?

Over the years, I have moved back and forth across the spectrum of the two extremes—complete tolerance and acceptance at one end and the expectations of typical behaviour at another. Through my own experiences and my conversations with many parents of autistic children, I have arrived at my current stance of 'setting the bar realistically high'.

I would not have come to this conclusion, however, if not for Yuri, my husband, who challenged me by setting high expectations for Sebastien, which were akin to those for a typical child. Even though I am the sole biological parent of my son, I realise that I could not have accomplished the task of bringing him up on my own during the early days.

I met Yuri, just two weeks after receiving the news of Sebastien's diagnosis. By that time, I had already been subject to the tyranny of Sebastien's rigid ways for three months. God only knows how long I would have gone on with this lifestyle of orchestrating my errands and the routes around his preferences before I was driven insane. Any deviations from these routine and routes led to tantrums such as rolling on the ground, arching his back and lurching his head to hit it on the ground, along with the relentless screaming and crying.

On my own, during the early days, I would have been willing to accommodate Sebastien and his sensitivities. It was just too tiring and too difficult to fight him all the time. However, Yuri, with his strength and staunch belief that Sebastien could not continue to impose his tyrannous ways on us and our lifestyle, set all of us free.

It was an uphill battle for the next two years. While Sebastien fought tooth and claw to live life on his terms, Yuri and I fought relentlessly over him. At the time, I thought Yuri's excessively high expectations of Sebastien smacked of his lack of knowledge of autism and understanding of what Sebastien could realistically be expected to do. I thought that his drive to expect Sebastien to be normal stemmed solely from his own motives of not wanting to be embarrassed in public by Sebastien—something that was ultimately trivial and inconsequential to me. From Yuri's perspective, I was spoiling Sebastien by cutting him too much slack and making too many excuses for him. One of my husband's earliest remarks about my mothering ability really hit me hard back then: "I am glad that you were not my mother when I was a child."

It took me four years to come to realise that Yuri's strict and rigid stance had its positive effects. With the benefit of hindsight, I had to admit to myself that I could not have raised an autistic child who could go out on family errands and excursions without warning or preparation; eat at any restaurant without throwing a fuss; and participate in activities in the crowded Las Vegas that is considered overly stimulating for typical people, let alone autistic children.

Through my conversations with other parents of autistic children, I have come to appreciate this achievement. Many of these parents limit their outings to their autistic child's favourite places such as specific restaurants. I knew a mother who got into a fight with her husband because he had dared to suggest that the entire family—their two typical daughters and autistic son—go to Las Vegas for a vacation. The fear of her son acting out in an unpredictable fashion in public was too mortifying and anxiety-provoking for her. This was a mother who devoted her life to ferrying her son from one therapy to another and who required the support of a behavioural therapist to take her son out to McDonald's—the treat for the week.

Sebastien's adjustment into the social world was by no means a smooth transition. Yuri and I, however, were willing to brave through these tantrums in order to have a life. As a result, we exposed Sebastien to frequent changes in his routines, thus succeeding in alleviating his rigid clinging to routines.

But it was no easy task during the early days. With his desperate and thus tyrannical adherence to routines and familiar places, Sebastien made any detours from routines a nightmare. For me, I had to brace myself for his adverse reactions each time I had to run errands that would take us out of the routine paths. I used to hate the thought of going to ATMs—something that was not part of Sebastien's routine, while knowing and anticipating with dread that he would lie in the middle of the pavement screaming, kicking and flailing his limbs. With Yuri's encouragement and admonitions, I went through these hard times, not knowing when they would end. Even though I never thought of it as a strategy, this approach ultimately paid off.

Of course, my recognition of Yuri's contributions does not mean that we have resolved our disagreements about how Sebastien should be raised. To this day, I continue to feel that my husband's expectations of typical behaviour from Sebastien are unrealistic at times. I had adjusted my previously low expectations for Sebastien through my battles with Yuri, however.

During those early days, Yuri looked beyond Sebastien and his disabilities to see a child who can participate in mainstream society and engage in certain activities without being undermined by his handicaps. He would often boast to me: "When you are not around and I am hanging out with him, he acts just like any other kid."

In spite of his boasts and exaggerations, what Yuri said had a modicum of truth. One day, I watched Sebastien helped Yuri to tighten the screws on a video recorder after Yuri fixed it. Although he was performing this action for the first time in his life, Sebastien was completely focused and attentive. Under Yuri's watchful eyes and minimal guidance, he was seemingly transformed into a typical child without any of his strange sounds and weird mannerisms.

Ultimately, Sebastien and I owe a lot to Yuri's uncompromising pursuit for normalcy for Sebastien early in our journey. By setting the bar so high for Sebastien at the time when the rest of us did not, Yuri showed more respect and faith in his ability and potential than anyone else in his life. These days, when I hear parents excusing their children's inappropriate behaviours or poor performance, I tell them: "Setting high, but realistic expectations, is a sign of respect for our children. Just because they have special needs does not mean that they cannot be expected to do anything." Thus, I was fortunate that Yuri was there, from the beginning, to teach me this important lesson.

Chapter Two

Running the Marathon of Raising an Autistic Child

In Search of the Miracle

One of the constant dilemmas confronted by parents of children with autism is whether we have done all that needs to be done to help our children attain normalcy. We are plagued, no, tormented by the incessant 'what if' questions:

What if there is a solution out there, which would help him to become normal?

What if this solution that miraculously cured so-and-so could help my son? And I did not try it?

What if?

For mothers who have decided to make their quest for these remedies their mission in life, this pursuit can rapidly consume all of their life, engulf their beings and leave them tossing and turning for many sleepless nights. Knowing mothers who feel burnt out after dealing with their children's autism for only one or two years, the peril of this course, like the hunt for a hidden treasure that may or may not exist out there, can be painfully evident from a bystander's perspective.

Yet, for these mothers caught up in this relentless quest, there does not seem to be any another choice. Heeding what the developmental experts say about the 'window period' of development, these mothers feel that they are trapped in a race against time. The closing of the window demarcates the decrease in the possibilities of hope with the inevitable passage of time.

Up against these odds, it is little wonder that these parents are running at top speed, trying to go as fast as they can during the early years, even as their bodies strain for air and their minds yearn for a measure of respite. But they cannot genuinely rest because they are propelled by the feelings of guilt that are fuelled by the 'what if' questions. For them, there is no pausing for a single moment to ponder the underlying treachery of the 'what if' questions that can lead them into an endless maze that offers no means of escape. Because the treachery of the questions lies in their promise of an imminent end—the happy ending—though no specific date is provided.

The truth is—this quest to help our children to attain normalcy, to be typical—is deceptive. For what is 'typical' in the eyes of these mothers? 'Typical', as defined by the milestones of the developmental experts, only describes an abstract child that does not really exist in real life. More importantly, what does 'typical' look like for each of our children with all their unique characteristics, in spite of their common diagnosis? This elusive quest for normalcy can thus be a self-perpetuating nightmare: When should we stop and declare that 'enough is enough' without feeling the weight of the 'what if' questions pushing us to go on?

Although I am not one of these mothers whose entire existence revolves around their children, I too, have been caught up in the feverish swirl of the 'what if' questions whenever the latest fad comes into town. I am confronted by these fads as I sit in the waiting rooms of the therapy facilities and hear mothers passing on stories and spreading the news. Then, I am tormented by my inability to pay for the treatments, or my unwillingness to subject my son to the treatments. The 'what if' questions spin in my head day and night until I make the decision either to do it or not to do it by asking the people I know and trust for their opinions. Only when I have made the decision and come to terms with them will I begin to enjoy my son again, instead of living in my fortress of swirling questions.

A wise woman once said, "Raising a child with autism is like running a marathon. You have to pace yourself, or you will burn out. There are many years ahead of you." I do not remember her name. She was a speaker, on the panel at the Autism Society of America Conference in Los Angeles, who was not a famous expert or a celebrated person with autism. She was a middle-aged gray-haired woman with autism who imparted her gem of wisdom in a flat and monotonous voice. Her expressionless eyes further distanced by her eyeglasses belied the fact that she had just spoken words of tremendous significance.

Apart from being a person with autism, she had also spent her life raising her two children with autism. Unlike any other experts, she possessed the piercing insight that could have only been gained by someone who had experienced both sides of the fence.

Her words of infinite wisdom, delivered in her deadpan voice, penetrated deeply into my heart. Hearing them, I suddenly felt an overwhelming urge to cry. It was a relief to hear someone who understood and who had been on this journey. She had given me the permission to get off the crazy treadmill of chasing after every potential cure.

Ultimately, by investing our entire being in the quest for miracles, we can often miss out on the fundamental truth that the goal of the quest is not about discovering the miracle cure, but this journey of love that a parent has for a child. At the end of the day, we will lose sight of our child when our eyes are constantly directed at the distant horizon, instead of what is right in front of us.

While I write these words, I am reminded of how I had often forgotten that gem of wisdom to leap back onto the treadmill. Although the early years are often the hardest days for parents who have to overcome their feelings of shock and grief, the middle years are also very difficult. As the journey stretches on and our children present behaviours of increasing complexity, our spirit can grow weary and the prospect of a miracle cure can look ever more tempting.

The next series of essays document my 'middle years' when Sebastien was between five and eight.

Ten Steps Forward, Five Steps Back
(Phoenix, August 2004)

Progress in an autistic child can be a double-edged sword. While your child may be making progress in one area, it may be coupled with regressions in other areas. I have heard many mothers speak of similar experiences. In one case, a high-functioning seven-year-old autistic girl I knew who was making academic progress in school regressed completely in the area of toilet training. Although it was a milestone she had reached several years ago, the girl began to soil her pants out in the garden, instead of going to the bathroom, for the next two years.

In the case of Sebastien, his slowly budding language ability at the age of five was accompanied by a deterioration of his personality as he began to engage in acts of aggression. Although it had taken him nine arduous months of discrete trials and training to finally understand the concept of imitating sounds, it did not take long before this once docile child began to engage in aggression. Within a week, I saw the initial signs of his aggression such as pinching and scratching. His unfortunate interactions with controlling and unresponsive educators in the kindergarten further led to the escalation of his repertoire of aggressive actions to biting, hitting and kicking.

During that first week, I would not have predicted that his aggression would accelerate at a far greater pace than his progress in speech. Essentially, in my reckoning, Sebastien had taken one tiny step forward in the department of speech and one gigantic stride backwards in the social department. At that time, I felt cheated, as though I had made a deal with the devil—language and aggression vs. no language and docility.

As a parent of a child with special needs, I feel that experiences with regressions of any kind can be extremely devastating to all parents of autistic children. It has already taken a lot for us to be resigned to the fact that our autistic children will only be inching forward in their lives, even as their typical peers surge ahead, with their progress measured in mileage. From our perspective, our children can ill afford to go backwards. Thus, these backward movements are very hard to stomach.

Our investment in our children's progress can so absorb our energy and emotions that sometimes, the tiniest of setbacks can bring us down. For example, one day, when I was unable to get Sebastien (who was seven at the time) to put on a wristband—an all-day pass at the Adventuredome at Circus Circus Hotel, I was reduced to tears. Before this debacle, I had only been concerned that he would be too frightened to sit on the rides. What I was not prepared for was his resistance to even wear the wristband. I felt defeated before the real battle had begun. To me, it was a big stride backwards in my effort to initiate him into the children's world of entertainment. For the next 30 minutes, I left him alone to watch the rides, while I sat slumped in a bench, fighting back the tears and wallowing in self pity. I had to fight the urge to be angry with him.

So, you may wonder what keeps me going, even though there are days when I feel like I am wandering around in circles—days that often stretch into weeks and even months. If you ask me what motivates me about taking those baby steps forward and backwards with Sebastien, I could tell you it is because I have no other choice, because giving up is not an option. The real truth is that I do not give up because Sebastien does not give up. Even as he takes the baby steps forward and backwards, he keeps going.

I am reminded of his perseverance in August 2004 when I emerged from his room after completing our first real reading session—a storybook from cover to cover. Tracing his fingers across the page, Sebastien read a simple book about Barbie going to a fair, word for word, from cover to cover. He laboured over each word, looking up at me for help with almost every single word.

Listening to his voice slurry with minimal intelligibility, I could not help but feel suffused with overwhelming sadness—so much effort, so little result. Anyone else hearing us reading the book would have wondered, "What was the point of it all?" After all, the child was barely comprehensible and needed so much assistance for simple words. In truth, anyone who was performing the task that poorly would have thrown his hands up in the air and given up in frustration.

To be honest, I wanted to give up and call it a night. The fact that he had tried to read was good enough for me. It just felt too hard and too tiring to keep plodding till the end of the book. Since I was the one who initiated the reading of the book, I wanted to give him the option to stop reading the book. So I asked him, "All done with book?" He protested, "No no no no," as though I were taking away his favorite toy. Anyone who knows Sebastien will know that books do not fall under the category of his favourite toys by any stretch of the imagination.

To make sure that I understood him, Sebastien held tightly onto my fingers to point at each word as he turned the page to start the painstaking reading of another page. With his firm grip on my fingers and his steady movement across the page, he communicated his desire and determination to finish reading the book. Then I knew, for certain, that he wanted to read the book!

To understand the momentousness of this event, let me just say that if you had told me a month ago that my son and I would be reading a book together, I would have laughed hysterically. Sebastien was a child who could not sit still enough to listen to 'a reading of the book'. His sole interaction with books was flipping pages quickly to the end, or fixating on a particular page that contained images of a train or anything else he liked, which meant that no other pages of the book would even be seen. In short, Sebastien did not read, at least, not in the traditional sense of the word.

Nonetheless, that night, as painful as we sounded to any objective outsider, or to my ears, we read at a plodding pace. To me, our reading session was a miracle, a triumph, a 'wonder moment'. When we finally made it to the end of the book, I complimented Sebastien with applause and a 'high five'. He applauded with me and gave me a 'high five', but without marked enthusiasm. To him, it was clearly not a momentous event. He did not seem to think much of his effort.

Then, the reason underlying his nonchalance dawned on me. For him, reading the book was just one of the many difficult and challenging tasks that he had had to struggle through to complete. Having to persevere and struggle was just part and parcel of his daily existence. For him, it was truly no big deal. After almost eight years of doing this, he was a veteran. Because of his disability, he is constantly forced to step out of his comfort zone, to step up to the plate to do something that is difficult for him.

Even as I was saddened by his belaboured reading, it was hard not to feel a surge of pride—a mother's pride of the accomplishments of her child. While most people feel a sense of pride when their children do something better than most people can, I am proud when I see Sebastien accomplish virtually anything because I know how hard it is for him, even though it may be something that is easily accomplished by others.

Thus, I am once again reminded of what keeps me going on this arduous journey of raising a child with autism. The journey can be analogised to our reading of the Barbie book. Though the going may be rough and seemingly pointless at times, I know the road is far harder for Sebastien than it is for me. His indomitable spirit and his unwillingness to give up keep me going. Today, I can see that he persisted in finishing the book, not because he enjoyed reading it, but because he was driven to complete this task. Giving up, to him, was not an option.

Taking a step back from his day-to-day existence, I can see that Sebastien's progress is only apparent when you look back across the space of time—all the way back to the starting point and then seeing where he is today. Then, you look at him at all the different points in between. Only with this non-linear perspective can you truly see and appreciate the painstaking progress that he has made. Like the tortoise in the famous fable, slow but steady. This is how I rise above my frustration each day and acknowledge that progress has been made. It is simply a matter of shifting one's perspective. In reality, Sebastien's progress far exceeds his regressions. At the end of the day, it is ten steps forward and five steps back, not the other way round.

The Rude Awakening
(Phoenix, January 2005)

For the last two years, after utilising everything that I had learned from occupational therapists, behaviourists, speech therapists and teachers, I had begun to feel like a veteran. Although I would not consider myself to be on cruise control with regard to raising Sebastien, I considered myself to be somewhat of a seasoned veteran in managing his challenging behaviours, especially in public. Many parents dread taking their children out to the public, especially to an unfamiliar and an uncontrolled setting for fear that their children would act out in an uncontrollable manner. Unlike these parents, I had thought that I had all the tricks up my sleeve to cover the wide repertoire of Sebastien's behaviours and nip them in their bud— a confidence that I had built up over the years of bad experiences and surviving them. Or so I had thought...

My rude awakening occurred more than a month after I decided to embark on the quest for a miracle. After moving to Phoenix from Los Angeles, I sought to learn about my new home and forge new social networks by joining a support group for parents of children with autism. Upon the recommendations of these mothers who all claim that their children were thriving and talking because of the gluten-free (no wheat) and casein-free (no dairy) diet (GFCF diet), my mind began spinning the 'what if' questions again—wondering and fantasising. From these enthusiastic mothers who supplied me with plenty of information from their experiences and their doctors, I was aware that Sebastien's behaviour would at first deteriorate, though it would subsequently improve dramatically, along with his other cognitive and social abilities. At the time, I felt confident enough to handle anything he might throw at me.

After the first three weeks, amidst some minor improvements in his attention span, I saw clear signs of behavioural problems. I justified and explained them away, however. I attributed his increasing unwillingness to comply with my instructions to his growing maturity ("After all, he is already eight years old."). I accounted for his obsessive and compulsive attachment to routines to the periodic fluctuations of his behaviour ("That's how he is. It comes and goes."). I blamed his seeming inability to control his negative emotions, particularly his outbursts of aggression in the public space against children who provoked him, on the naughty typical children who pushed his buttons ("Sebastien was lashing out because he could not talk."). Essentially, I was desperate for the GFCF diet to give me the miracle.

One week later, however, came even more troubling reports from school—Sebastien came home with a scratch on his cheek, near his eye that was a result of his failed attempt to attack his speech pathologist with a pencil. While his aggression was no surprise to me, the lack of a reason underlying his attack—typically, frustration with school work or a change in routine—was extremely puzzling. The speech pathologist said that they had just barely sat down and she had given him an unchallenging task, after hearing that he had attacked a child earlier in the morning for no apparent reason. According to her, it appeared as though Sebastien could not help himself. I did not buy her story. There was always a reason. I blamed the teachers for not observing him closely and for not determining the root cause.

At the same time, I was troubled. A storm was brewing in the horizon and it was approaching furiously. By then, Sebastien's aggression that had been extinguished at home broke out as he not only tried to attack me, but also Yuri, who had not been touched during his previous episode of aggression three years earlier. Still, I was unconvinced. Not for a moment did I think that his behaviour could be a result of the GFCF diet.

I was forced to examine the effects of the GFCF diet on my son during our regular Las Vegas vacation one week later. After going there for the last six years, going to Las Vegas for a vacation was a treat for the entire family. For Sebastien, the place was replete with wonders: the endless glass elevators and the escalators along the strip; the magnificent Manhattan roller coaster at the New York New York Hotel; the musical fountains of the Bellagio Hotel; the terrifying, yet fascinating, dolphins that cavort playfully in the pool; and the exhilarating and stimulating motion rides.

Through repeated exposure, Sebastien had become successful at coping with the sensory challenges presented by Las Vegas. With its teeming crowds, long lines at rides and buffets, the lights and the sounds of the slot machines ringing away, the unintelligible chatter of people at the gambling tables, the cries of unhappy and fatigued children, along with the uninhibited exclamations of winners and partygoers who are already drunk by noon, Las Vegas can be a sensory nightmare for anyone, especially to one who is autistic. By the time we were in Las Vegas for the ill-fated vacation, however, Sebastien had become a huge fan of Las Vegas and would inevitably cry when it was time to bid farewell to this city.

That time, Sebastien, the seasoned veteran of Las Vegas, who had become accustomed to the long lines and the need to change plans because of unanticipated renovations or schedule changes, simply fell apart. Any deviations from his routines and his expectations transformed him into an inconsolable wreck. Then, without warning, he would whip out his hand to claw at my hand, or pinch me, just to vent his overwhelming feelings of disappointment.

Shocked at his unexpected behaviour, I reached into my bag of strategies and implemented them on the first day. I sat him down and verbally reprimanded him in a harsh voice, until he expressed remorse and repentance in the form of tears—my method to ensure that he understood that I was displeased with him. This time, however, the tears simply translated into more aggression—against any unsuspecting passers-by. With his anger and disappointment still simmering inside behind his expressionless facade, he lashed out his arm to grab at anyone by the arm.

Seeing Sebastien hitting out at strangers, as though he were seemingly unable to inhibit his impulsive urges that were engulfing his being, I felt sick at heart. All the years of helping him to adjust to life in the public space had come down to this. In one day, all my confidence and my pride disintegrated in the face of a horrifying fear that he had transformed into a monster, a wild beast that could not be tamed. Each time he hit out at me, I could see his beautiful face marred by the vicious snarl of his mouth, the baring of his teeth and the sharp glint of his hardened eyes. While these moments were fleeting in real time and seemed surreal in retrospect, their occurrence would haunt me for many months after his aggression was overcome.

How could I properly describe the scene that first day of the nightmarish vacation in Las Vegas? There we were walking down Las Vegas Boulevard, with the sidewalks spilling over with tourists walking in both directions. I trudged purposely down the sidewalk, threading my way through this mass of humanity—their bodies all potential targets for Sebastien's unpredictable assaults of pinches, grabs and hits. So I held onto his wrists, using my two hands as though they were handcuffs to prevent him from inflicting harm on others with his hands. Even as I invested every ounce of my energy in thwarting him from hurting others, I was thinking that he might resort to biting me then when one of his weapons of choice—his hands—was unavailable.

That night, I felt no sense of reprieve, even after making it back to the hotel room, without anyone else falling prey to Sebastien's unexpected assaults. For me, there was only the horrible aftermath of trying to figure out what went wrong and what strategies I should implement, while struggling to keep my fears and sadness at bay.

After putting Sebastien to bed, I sat in the bathroom and stared at my tear-stained reflection in the bathroom mirror. Amidst the spinning thoughts and feelings raging in my mind, I managed only to utter a silent prayer: "I just want my baby back."

The next day, deducing that his dramatic changes in behaviour were likely due to the GFCF diet, I fed him his favourite cinnamon Wetzel pretzel and a big scoop of vanilla ice cream. Never in my life have I seen him devoured food so quickly and enthusiastically. Although I wished otherwise, I realised that I could not change his behaviours within the next few days, even if I fed him all the flour and dairy products he could possibly eat.

So, over the next few days, I continued to witness his displays of aggression and confronted the scary spectre of him as a young man wreaking havoc on society. In the face of the ugliness of his behaviour, I thought about the day—the inevitable day when he will be physically stronger than I am and I can no longer hold onto his wrists. Although I have learnt over the years not to think too far ahead in my journey, this eerie spectre of his future was a rude awakening for me. In the months ahead, as I fought hard to free him from his addiction to the power of aggression, my love for him would be even more severely tested.

So what did I learn from this experience?

At the time, I had thought that my selection of the GFCF diet among the many radical biomedical options for Sebastien was relatively harmless. After experiencing the consequences, I became acutely aware of the awesome responsibility I bear as a parent of an autistic child who cannot speak up on his own. Essentially, in pursuing cures, remedies and solutions to pursue a miracle, we, as parents may forget that we are treating our children as guinea pigs. Though it may not be our intention, we do take the risk of wreaking havoc with their bodies and their minds.

To be fair, we parents are bombarded by a dizzying array of choices and options, many promising to elicit miraculous results, with none offering the certainty of such an outcome. Very often, we feel overwhelmed by the sheer weight of making difficult decisions. In going with the GFCF diet, I based my judgment on what others said, not on my instincts. I was simply caught up by the possibility of Sebastien being transformed by the diet. This reckless pursuit of the miraculous cure blew up in my face.

This episode, with its lingering consequences, served as a powerful reminder to me that I have been entrusted with my son's body and his mind. Because he does not have the voice or the words to protest, he is even more vulnerable than the average child to external manipulations and interventions.

Still, Sebastien managed to communicate to me. The raw and instinctual aggression that erupted from his being spoke to me loud and clear. It would not have been the first time that he had had to rely on his aggression to communicate to the rest of the world. I can only hope that, one day, he would discover other means of communication to make me listen.

(NOTE: This essay is, in no way, a blanket criticism of GFCF diet. Many parents of autistic children who have implemented this diet have considered it to be effective for their children. When I shared my experience of the GFCF diet on an online support group for parents in Phoenix, other parents also highlighted similar experiences with their children. So it is a diet that may work for some children, but not for others.)

Profiling Sebastien's Aggression
(Phoenix, February 2005)

Aggression in an autistic child can take on a most deceptive guise. From the perspective of understanding specialists and educators in this field, aggression stems from the autistic child's inability to communicate. Autistic children hit out because they are frustrated by their inability to express themselves, particularly their emotions. While it is fine for a group of specialists sitting in the conference room to arrive at this conclusion, the prospect of being at the mercy of my son's aggression until the day he can communicate appropriately was not something that I was prepared to live with after my experience in Las Vegas.

The first time I had ever encountered an autistic child acting in an aggressive fashion was at a domestic violence shelter for battered women and their children. Even though Sebastien was already in my life then, he was still an infant and his diagnosis was still months away. At the shelter, there was a five-year-old African American child whom we were simply told was autistic. He was unable to talk. Because of his disruptive behaviour, he did not attend school with his older brother and the other typical kids at the shelter.

None of the women at the shelter had ever dealt with an autistic child before. One female volunteer in her sixties experienced tremendous difficulties with him. In one instance, the little boy bit her, as she tried to force the child to stop playing and go into the house for a snack. This woman had tried to drag the resistant child out of the room, while he was in the middle of playing with a toy, without initial efforts to coax him or speak to him. Because he was unsuccessful in extricating his hand from her grasp, he bit her wrist. She let go of him instantly, while unleashing a torrent of abuse at him. I will never forget the look of pure hatred that she hurled at him. In retrospect, with my experience of being a mother of an autistic child, I felt for the misunderstood young boy.

Little would I know that five years later, I would be dealing with another five-year-old who was prone to aggression. This time, he was my son. Sebastien's first descent into aggression when he was five years old would follow a similar trajectory, except within a different setting—a special needs kindergarten classroom. He also resorted to aggression in an attempt to get away from a one-on-one aide who was relentless in holding onto him. To make her life easier, the aide figured that she would simply hold onto Sebastien's hand to help him complete all the worksheets assigned to him—most of which were beyond his level. Essentially, this woman tried to control Sebastien's every move by holding onto him in order to ensure that he would behave appropriately and not disrupt the classroom. Whether he was actually learning anything or not was rather unimportant to her.

During my observation of him, I saw that Sebastien would tolerate her hand-over-hand behaviour while they were working at the table for a period of 45 minutes. When she continued to wrap her arms around him during Circle Time when the children move from the table to the carpeted floor, however, he would explode. When pulling away only led to her holding him tighter, he pinched and bit her. The success of these measures of aggression illuminated their awesome power and effectiveness in getting him what he wanted quickly. In his first cycle of aggression, Sebastien definitely utilised it as a communication tool to get away from his insensitive and oppressive one-on-one aide.

In my mind, there is no question that Sebastien's aggression started out as a communication issue. I recognised the communicative function of aggression, particularly for those who lack a conventional means of interaction and communication with others. But more importantly, for Sebastien, I saw that aggression was also very attractive because it gave him the power to exercise his will and demand respect for his wishes. He was essentially sending a powerful message to people: 'Just because I am unable to speak does not entitle you to impose your wishes on me.'

When it first erupted at the age of five, Sebastien's aggression revealed a side of him that had lain dormant for two years when he was unable to utter any sounds at all. The explosion of his aggression illuminated that he had possessed pent-up fury at his inability to communicate his needs and wants with the outside world. In spite of his mask of indifference and docility, he held onto tremendous anger at us adults who often manipulated his body and forced him to do things against his will in the different therapeutic interventions. Because he was non-verbal, it had just been easier to physically move him, instead of waiting for him to respond appropriately.

After too much 'manhandling' in that kindergarten classroom, however, Sebastien who had previously displayed no problems with physical handling, no longer wanted people to pull him, shift him from spot to spot, or move his limbs without his desire. In fact, it got to the point when people, particularly children, who were in his vicinity, were potential targets, simply because they stood too close to him. That was when I saw a completely different aspect of his aggression. To me, it was clearly more than a communication issue.

I decided that aggression, in the hands of a child with autism, is ultimately about the need for control and power. To me, Sebastien's aggression that was initially born out of the desperate attempt to assert oneself, to fend for oneself, took on a life of its own. Whatever he experienced in that classroom began to spill into all the other areas of his life. In fact, he came to view his aggression as a game of cause and effect that fed his sense of power.

Through his aggression, Sebastien discovered a power that he delighted in. For once, he possessed the tool that he could use to manipulate the world, just as he had been manipulated. During our walks to and from home, he attempted to pinch me for the fun of it. Back then, without a real strategy for dealing with his relentless attacks, I raced down the streets in an attempt to elude his attacks so that he could not have the satisfaction of succeeding. It was a game that I did not want him to win. If I managed to escape, however, innocent passers-by often served as satisfactory substitutes.

Like a willful child, he exulted in the power of his brand new 'toy'. He brandished it without knowing its meaning, its consequences and its outcomes. All he knew was that it triggered an effect that he wanted. It made people leave him alone when they bothered him too much. Moreover, he was able to trigger reactions in people, when they yelped in pain.

Little did he know that he was as much controlled by his aggression as he thought he was controlling it. In reality, Sebastien's body had gotten so tense and stressed and his being had gotten so addicted to the use of aggression as a means of unleashing his stress that he resorted to aggression towards all people, including those whom he liked.

The first time round, it took three months before Sebastien's rampant aggression subsided. It involved the replacement of the one-on-one woman aide with a male aide who was infinitely more sensitive to his needs and moods than the previous one. In the home setting, we discovered a behavioural strategy with the help of a behaviourist. Determining that the precursor to his aggression was his 'meany' face—the jutting of his chin and the gnawing of his teeth—we halted the momentum of his aggression by issuing the command: "No meany face." It was a strategy that would prove to be deceptively simple and effective for the next three years. With the effective and consistent implementation of this strategy, aggression was completely eliminated at home.

His aggression, though attenuated, remained in other settings such as the school, however. At school, educators who were considerably distracted by multiple children and tasks often failed to catch Sebastien's 'meany' faces. More often than not, they chose to ignore these early signs (in spite of my warnings and suggestions) until they escalated into actual aggression. In addition, Sebastien was also frustrated by the learning tasks given to him, which were meaningless or too difficult for him. Although children with special needs were supposed to have an individualised curriculum, that was seldom the case. In reality, educators and aides were not trained properly, nor were they given sufficient time and support to truly develop individualised learning tasks for each of the children in the class.

At that juncture, I still decided that we had been effective in eliminating Sebastien's aggression. In other words, if all the adults were to implement my 'no meany face' strategy and placed realistic expectations on him, Sebastien would not have an aggression problem. Even though I knew that the germ of aggression still lay within him, because it would erupt in spurts whenever the opportunities arose, particularly in schools, I let these episodes slide, because they were isolated episodes with no apparent connections. I simply placed pressure on the teachers to catch those 'meany faces'.

Cruising along with this approach for three years, I was totally unprepared for the evolution of Sebastien's aggression that was triggered by the GFCF diet when he turned eight. Even after he was off the diet for a few weeks, his aggression did not stop. Rather, his aggression took on an entirely different character than before. For a start, his external acts of aggression did not begin and end with the triggering event. An event that was traumatic for him, such as a visit to the dentist, could trigger aggression that lasted for weeks and months, as though he could never vent the full extent of his fury. Moreover, every little thing including dropping a pencil on the floor could set him off.

Not knowing how to deal with his current version of aggression, I had to reframe my perspective of Sebastien's aggression. No longer was I willing to make excuses for his aggression because of his inability to communicate. While his aggression might have started out as his desperate attempt to assert himself, there was no getting around the reality that aggression equals aggression.

In reaching this chilling conclusion, I felt that I had finally moved past the euphemistic guise of Sebastien's aggression to acknowledge the traumatic effects of his aggression on me as his mother. During this difficult period of coping with his aggression on a daily basis, I was physically affected—the tightening of my belly; the dryness in my throat; the furious pounding of my heart; my hyper-reaction to every move he made especially in the public space; the fear of touching him; and the constant need to anticipate his act of aggression.

At that juncture, the 'no meany face' approach had lost complete effectiveness because Sebastien showed no signs of aggression on his face. One moment his expression was flat, the next, he had lunged and attacked someone. The timing of the 'meany' face coincided with his 'meany act'!

As a mother, it was not the pain of the attacks that hurt me the most. What really got me were the sudden occurrence of these attacks and the sudden transformation of his features. Essentially, I was on my toes all the time, anticipating and dreading for the inevitable moment to arrive for the day, wondering whether it would be the first and only one, or the precursor to a bad day of multiple episodes.

None of the raw terror of aggression is ever captured within the sterility of the Individualised Education Plan (IEP) meetings held annually at the school. In fact, it was so easy, in the civilised setting, to transform the reality of Sebastien's aggression into a communication problem. During the previous three years, I had taken the term 'communication problem' and run away with it.

As I watched Sebastien's proclivity towards aggression in horror, however, I came to realise the error of this approach. By failing to call aggression by its name, I had taught him, as with the specialists, to think that he was entitled to be aggressive whenever he felt anger and frustration. It was a mistake to simply try to prevent him from experiencing the feelings that could lead to anger. For the last three years, we had focused on preventing him from feeling frustrated in our aggression strategy. When his aggression reared its ugly head in school, I just blamed the teachers and aides for failing to catch his meany face in time, or for giving him work that was too hard for him.

In reality, his aggression problem should have been likened to a person who cannot control his anger. He had become a bully. Though his aggression might have stemmed from the fact that he was a 'special needs child' with a communication issue, it was no longer a special needs issue. He had simply become a bully who used his aggression to get what he wanted.

So often, in fighting very hard to make accommodations for our 'special needs children', we may sometimes miss the obvious facts of their problematic behaviours. In wanting others to bend backwards to give special treatment to our children, however, we are not necessarily doing them a favour. For one thing, we are not helping them to survive in this world—a world that will not necessarily be so forgiving of some of the hurtful actions of our children. As advocates for our children's needs, we must also not blind ourselves to the realities of our children and their inappropriate behaviours. When their behaviours are unacceptable, we must step up to the plate as parents, to show them a better way. As for me, I certainly did not expect the world to bend backwards for Sebastien and put up with his aggression. Out of love and respect for him, I could not afford to do so anymore.

In order to extinguish the aggression once and for all, I decided to crack down on it by separating Sebastien's frustration from his aggression. I did not know why it took me so long to realise this simple truth: All of us get frustrated, upset and angry, but we do not unleash our negative emotions by engaging in aggression. If frustration and anger is not a good justification for a typical individual to hit out at the world, why should we make a special case for a child with autism, or any other types of special needs?

So for the last three years, I had cultivated Sebastien's belief that his aggression was a justifiable consequence of his feelings of frustration and aggression. I had deluded myself into thinking that I could control his world and make sure that all the caregivers did the right thing. The truth was that at no time was I able to control his increased awareness of his deficits and his difficulties with the outside world, his reaction to the GFCF diet, or the unkindness of the people in the outside world. By trying to control the outside environment and preventing him from getting in touch with his negative emotions, I had shortchanged him by failing to teach him the one vital lesson that he had to learn: Aggression is not acceptable, no matter how badly he feels or how justified his response.

My realisation and adjustment of my perspective was only the beginning of my difficult journey. I still had to formulate and implement new strategies that would help me to convey my lesson successfully to Sebastien who was by then so intoxicated with the power of aggression. Warding away the prospect of giving him a pharmaceutical drug to alleviate his aggressive impulses, I conceived a multi-pronged approach to deal with his aggression at different levels.

First of all, to help him take control of his rising feelings of frustration and anger, I tried to show him techniques for alleviating his negative feelings. At first, I tried to teach him to breathe deeply. He could not grasp the concept of breathing, however. So, in the end, I decided to teach him to count from 'one to ten' the moment he felt 'meany'.

Then, in order to decrease the attractiveness of aggression to him, I meted out negative consequences to hold him accountable for his actions. Knowing how attached he was to the toys in his room, which were arranged in specific formations, I threatened and subsequently removed them for each act of transgression. At the same time, I celebrated and acknowledged his triumphs by returning the toys to the room when he achieved an 'aggression-free' day. Playing the role of the judge, I utilised his calendar to create a reward-consequence system. At the end of the day, I decided whether he would get a sad face that represented his aggression, or a star for aggression-free behaviour.

For parents who think that I may be treating my son harshly by resorting to these measures, I would defend myself by saying that I wished that I could be the loving parent who did not need to use harsh words, take away his toys and make him cry. If my unwillingness to crack down on his aggression meant that he would go out to the public space and hurt others, however, I would have failed him as a parent.

Although I put up a strong facade, even in the face of his tears and his protests, I too, was weeping inside. More than he could possibly imagine, I was saddened by the need to implement such measures. In retrospect, I think I felt like a parent who had been backed into a corner. By then, I had been a horrified witness of the eruption of his aggression one too many times. Each time his aggression occurred, my heart would shatter into a thousand pieces. Still, I held it together by going through the motions of implementing my behavioural approach and meting out the consequences of scolding him and taking away his toys.

During those early days of dealing with his most recent bout of aggression, I was ultimately strengthened by my belief that in setting high standards of behavior for him, in refusing to make excuses for his aggression, I was testing my faith in his ability to exercise his intelligence and his courage to rise above his challenging circumstances. I sincerely believed that when I respected him enough to expect him to do better than vent his feelings in aggression, I was guiding him out of the prison of his aggression. In spite of his deficits and his inability to assert his will and his desire for independence, Sebastien had to believe that there was another way—a path away from aggression.

James Redfield's *The Celestine Prophecy* to the Rescue (Phoenix, March 2005)

Two months into the implementation of my multi-pronged approach, I was teetering on the brink of utter despair. Although his aggression was lessening, its simmering presence underneath the surface was unmistakable, waiting for the right moment to reveal itself. At this point, I could see that Sebastien had replaced the traditional tantrum with his aggression. Confronted by the spectre of the presence of his aggression as a youth, I knew that I did not have the luxury for his aggression to linger on.

By then, the removal of toys had lost its sting. Sebastien simply got used to that reality as I upped the ante and removed three or four toys at a time. Then, when he had consecutive days of aggression, his room began to look decidedly empty, with very few precious things left for removal. My fierce reprimands that accompanied each removal of his toys only served to provoke him to greater anger that was repelled by my use of the spray bottle. Yes, by that time, I was using a spray bottle to repel him each time he lunged at me in anger. Nothing seemed to have a long-term effect. It was as though his anger and his desire for aggression were far greater than the pain of the adverse consequences. The two of us were trapped in a battle zone, with neither side willing to back down or make a change.

Most parents with 'special needs children' often find their information about autism in the massive corpus of works that have been published on the topic. In my case, I would discover my solution from a most unlikely source—James Redfield's *The Celestine Prophecy*. With its New Age philosophy and spirituality about life and human relationships, this book was a huge bestseller back when it was first published in 1993. Back then, I honestly could not grasp many of its esoteric principles and ideas. More than a decade later, however, I realised that it was a brilliant book that offered a perfectly logical and wonderful recipe of how people should treat one another.

More pertinently to my struggle with Sebastien's aggression, this book illuminated the fact that he and I were indeed engaged in a destructive power struggle, with each one of us vying to impose control over the other. I had to admit to myself that I was trying to impose my will on him, even when it was for his own good. In the same way that he was bullying me to get his way, I was also bullying him to get my way with all my strategies. I needed to replace the negative energy that was swirling around us with positive energy.

Inspired by this honest image of my relationship with Sebastien, I modified my disciplinary model. I still retained the counting from one to ten and the rewards-consequences system, however. Also, his aggression-free days were still celebrated with a star on his calendar, coupled with thunderous applause, big hugs and smiles.

I stopped the spray bottle approach and the scoldings. With the new system, I simply informed him every morning that I would deprive him of the the privileges and perks that he used to take for granted—his bed, his bubble bath (replaced by a shower, which is a far less appealing option for him), his night-time rice cracker snack (replaced by cereal, a secondary choice) and many of his toys—should he act 'meany' at school. I reminded him to count from one to ten when he felt mad and wanted to be 'meany' at school.

When he acted aggressively, whether at school or at home, I did not yell or scream at him. I would deliver my message to him in a calm and gentle voice: "I am so sorry, but you were meany today, now I would have to take away..."

The new system helped me to regain a sense of peace and sanity. More importantly, it wrought a transformation in Sebastien's behaviour. Stripped of the drama and the provocation of my scoldings, he accepted the removal of his privileges calmly and graciously, even though he was unhappy about them.

In retrospect, it would certainly have saved me a great deal of energy and angst to have instituted this system right away. Nonetheless, I was also aware of the fact that both of us had had to go through all the experimentation and the suffering to realise the wisdom of this approach. Sebastien had to embark on this long and challenging journey with me, for both of us to negotiate the nature of our relationship and to understand the inappropriateness of his aggression. It took time for him to understand why his privileges were taken away and the intricacies of the rule. Time was also needed for him to realise that the counting from one to ten was a tool to help him to assuage his frustration and aggression and integrate it into his daily repertoire. He had to learn to use it for himself, not to please me or others. The counting tool had to be meaningful for him.

I also needed to go through the struggle to come to terms with the reality that I could not impose my will on him, in spite of my best intentions. He needed time, space and peace to work things out for himself. His aggression was not something I could extract from his being through the sheer force of my will and my desire. I could not possibly try harder than he did to stop his aggression—it was something that he had to do for himself. With this perspective, I was able to step back, relax and guide him, without feeling the need to win the battle against his aggression. It was a battle that he must win for himself. I could only stand alongside him to provide him with guidance, support and love.

Who knows how long this system would last? All I know is that solutions can appear in the most unusual places. Mine came in the form of the Redfield book—a philosophical book about life encapsulated within the guise of an adventure novel—and it saved my life. And even though Sebastien did not even know of the book, it might have even saved his.

Chapter Three
Coming to Terms with Sebastien
to Fight the Good Fight

Fighting the Good Fight

I am a staunch believer in advocacy for our children. Years of living in the US has taught me that parents do a grave disservice to their autistic children when they do not advocate for them. Advocacy, however, is a particularly challenging issue for people from the Asian culture that prioritises collective harmony above individual needs. Parents in Asia often flinch from confrontations that need to arise when faced with unjust situations in which their children are taught or treated poorly. Coupled with the fact that parents often do not have many affordable educational and therapeutic options, they tend to swallow their unhappiness and dissatisfaction by compromising on the quality of care provided to their children.

When we do that, however, we are letting our children down and they, in turn, become disillusioned with us and the mainstream society. They feel let down by us. In some instances, this sense of disillusionment can lead to aggression, depression or other forms of self-destructive activities, especially when they grow older.

Just as significantly, parents may not fight for their children, simply because they perceive their children from the eyes of the outsider. Essentially, as typical individuals who follow social norms, they side with the teachers and others in judging their children's failure to comply with social expectations, without taking into consideration their children's deficits and challenges.

To fight the good fight for our children, we need to examine our own belief systems and our perceptions about our children. In order to become good advocates for them, we must first strive to see the world through their eyes, instead of our own. In the process, we can then begin to suspend our judgments and critical eyes to appreciate the efforts that they do to accommodate us and our world. Once we can grasp this fundamental fact, we can then properly represent our children and fight for them in mainstream society.

Understanding Sebastien and coming to terms with his weaknesses as well as his strengths, has transformed my perception of him. More than just a weak individual full of deficits, he is a strong and persistent boy who fights against all the odds to live in our world. This recognition of our autistic children as unique individuals, rather than deficient ones, is essential to enable us to know how to stand up for them.

Embracing Sebastien's Limitations
(Phoenix, April 2005)

What frustrates me more than anything in my journey with Sebastien is the realisation that even as he improves with passing time in his painstaking way, he is at the same time falling light years behind his peers in language, academic learning and social understanding. In a world that prizes winning and 'being the best' above all else, the celebration of the individual triumphs of the 'loser'—the individual who arrives last at the finishing line—is more the exception than the norm.

Thinking about this sad reality reminded me of the televised coverage of a swimming competition in the Commonwealth Games some years back, while I was still living in Australia. An hour or more after the winner had already completed the race, a lone swimmer from the country of the Isle of Man was still in the midst of completing the 3,000-metre race. A paltry number of the members of the audience had lingered on to watch and cheer for him. Although the competition was over and the outcome determined, he valiantly continued to swim even though it would have been easier just to quit. He swam on in order to achieve his personal best. That swimmer from the Isle of Man left an indelible impression on me, along with the small number of people who continued to cheer for him.

In many ways, Sebastien is very much like that lonesome swimmer from the Isle of Man. He competes against no one, because all the others are so far ahead that they are no longer in sight. And in the Olympics of our lives, I am the last, proud member of the audience who is cheering my heart out from the sidelines, waiting for Sebastien to complete the race and achieve his personal best however long it takes, even as the last of his supporters trickle away. I will always be the last audience member standing, ready to acknowledge his triumph. For him, there will be no loud applause, no frenzied cheering for his accomplishments. Only I will have known the effort he had undertaken, or can truly appreciate the magnitude of his accomplishments.

When observing Sebastien, you need to be willing to attend to the little things, every minutiae, because his accomplishments are not spectacular or extraordinary by conventional standards. Compared to a typical child, he often pales in comparison, so much so that for many years, he seemed to blend into the surroundings whenever there were typical children in the house. He was a silent being who drifted peripherally in the background, allowing the typical children to take over his domain, invade his space and play with his toys without any protest. He knew that he lacked the tools to compete successfully for attention.

Therefore, the only way to know that he has made any progress is to observe him closely. You have to register him doing things that he may have never been willing to try before; notice things that appear to be beyond his range of vision; plunge into activities that used to drive him away in fear; and interact with things he once ignored. I acknowledge and applaud all these improvements, even as I am painfully aware of how far away he is in terms of his development from his peers and even those who are far younger.

With Sebastien, I have had to constantly remind myself to let go of the 'what should be' expectations—that compulsive need of human beings to make comparisons and judge his performance. Only when I can manage to suspend that compulsive need to judge can I fully appreciate his uniqueness and his valiant attempt to cope with a world that is often too loud, over-stimulating, demanding, confusing and meaningless to him. In defense, he can only cover his ears, squeeze his eyes shut, run around the room or distract himself with his own activities.

Sometimes, it feels as though I am the sole witness of his efforts and his struggles to do his very best in this world. Because of this reality, I bear the responsibility of being Sebastien's voice in a world that does not understand his ways, recognise his strengths and see beyond his limitations. As I deal more and more with agencies and institutions that are supposed to help children with special needs and their families, I realise that I serve an important role of being Sebastien's interpreter.

For example, Sebastien was often subjected to a barrage of standardised tests each time he entered a new school, while we were living in the US. These standardised tests generally reduced him into a series of deficits and inadequacies. They measured how far behind he was, in comparison to a typical child. In my opinion, what was the point of the comparison? The fact that he lagged behind a typical child was painfully obvious to anyone. Even more significantly, an autistic child perceives, thinks and feels so differently from his or her typical counterpart that the comparison seems even more pointless.

At the end of the day, I find that I was the one who had to put back together the Sebastien that they had dissected in accordance with their discrete categories and criteria. My task was to ensure that they saw him as a whole person, despite his disability. I had to stick up for him and tell these experts that, in spite of their test results, they had gotten Sebastien all wrong.

No, he was not akin to a preschooler, even though he was an eight-year-old who could not make beyond two-word spontaneous utterances. No, he did not simply have an aggression or a communication issue. His aggression was a consequence of a person venting his frustration of living in a world in which he was never understood, in which his strengths were overshadowed by his weaknesses, in which he was judged by criteria that had little meaning to him. No, there are no standardised criteria or test scores, which can lead to the construction of an accurate representation of Sebastien.

Nonetheless, what remains the hardest thing for me is that I, the person who is closest to him, often do not have the slightest inkling of what is going on his head. Sometimes, when Sebastien sheds copious tears of sadness, I am unable to properly comfort him. He cannot respond to my questions of "Why? Why are you crying?"

These moments are tough because I cannot reach into the depths of his despair and help him deal with his emotions. They also remind me of how hard it is for him to live in our world. If I were him—an inhabitant in a land that does not speak his language—I believe that I too, would keep my most prized possession—my heart and my soul—tucked safely behind a mask of indifference to the outside world. The desire not to be hurt—surely we typical human beings should be able to understand that.

Yet we do not.

Conventional professionals in this field who are supposed to possess a vast store of knowledge about our children, with their strategies and techniques, medications and remedies, do not grasp this basic truth. Our children still bear the sense of humanity that is present within all of us. When we reduce autistic children to a series of check marks on instruments of measurement, we lose sight of their fundamental humanity. God only knows how typical people would appear to the discerning eye of the professional if we were described in terms of specific items on an instrument, based on 'how frequently' or 'how rarely' we do something.

In spite of my empathy towards Sebastien and my motherly bias, I used to shudder at the reality that I am his representative, as though I could truly read his mind and fathom the depths of his thoughts and emotions (though in truth, I only dance at the periphery). I knew that I had to do it, however, because I was the one who had to fill out these forms and instruments that consist of the myriad of items in which his behaviour was measured on a Likert scale of one to five so that the experts could rate him with a number and interpret him based on this number. It was a job I did so that Sebastien could receive the necessary services, but I did not believe for a second that they accomplished anything in helping him. Therefore, the more I listened to these experts talk about him behind their facade of expertise, the more I realised that if there were anyone who understood him, perhaps, I came the closest, even though I would always remain a person on the fringe.

The truth is, what I genuinely think and feel about Sebastien are, unfortunately, things that we did not share at those annual IEP meetings in schools. In fact, it would be a travesty to talk about something so precious and intimate within the school office, surrounded by people who care about your child with limitations.

This is how I see Sebastien: I consider him to be my guiding light, the centre of my soul. Although it feels vulnerable to have the foundation of one's being lodged in that of an autistic child, therein lies the truth of my existence and my vulnerability. I draw comfort and sustenance from his uniqueness and strength. The whiny sounds he makes as he runs a marker along his roller coaster; his endless efforts at rearranging his bedsheet over his mattress; his luscious and expressive eyes that speak a thousand words and try to compensate for his lack of verbal speech; and his passion for living provide me with the energy and the will to trudge on, to see the light at the end of the tunnel.

Most of all, Sebastien inspires me with his perseverance. Here is a child who gets up each day to face a world in which he has no means of communication, in which he is isolated and alone, in which the number of his failures far exceeds his successes. He messes up time and time again and falls down almost everyday. Yet he gets up over and over again.

Each morning, when I open the door, he pops his little head out of his covers and greets me and the day with his dazzling smile.With his bright twinkling eyes, he lets me know—"I am ready to go. I am ready to take on the world for another day." Somehow, Sebastien has the right attitude about life, which often escapes the typical person. Undaunted by life's challenges, he is willing to tackle them with a passion and enthusiasm unmatched by most people I know.

Living in a world that can at times feel cold, lonely and unresponsive to the plight of the individual, I often turn to Sebastien during these dark moments. I look at him and I am renewed by the purity of his spirit—one that does not judge people by the colour of their skin, the amount of money they possess, or their beauty that lies skin-deep. And then suddenly, the world is not such a cold and lonely place after all. That is the Sebastien I know and cherish, and the one that the experts will never know.

Sanctuary
(Phoenix, April 2005)

Parents of autistic children often impose excessive pressure on their autistic children by failing to give them a respite from all the educational and therapeutic programmes in their lives. Wanting their children to learn at all times and catch up, these parents fail to recognise the importance of providing their children with a sanctuary.

In my definition, a 'sanctuary' is simply a time period and space in which autistic children can simply be who they are. Within this sanctuary, autistic children should be allowed to engage in behaviours that may look odd to the outside world such as hand flapping or crashing into cushions. Our children need a respite from the continuous scrutiny and judgment they encounter throughout the rest of the day. These moments in the sanctuary are vital in helping them to be successful in their other endeavours.

Although I expect Sebastien to behave properly in public by setting a high standard for him, I let him make his funny noises, play with his toys in his own strange way and create his unusual routines within the confines of his room. To me, he needs to be given a sanctuary, a space of his own, or a haven for him to be as 'autistic' as he wants to be. In his sanctuary, he should be free from the expectations of the outside world, as well as their endless corrections and criticisms. It offers him a break from the mainstream world where he seems to fall short each and every time, before he even opens his mouth, acts, or makes a move. In his sanctuary, he can do no wrong because in this space, he is in complete control.

I doubt that my husband, Yuri, would agree with me about this aspect. After all, there is much to be said for consistency in eradicating 'unwanted' behaviours. Yet in the depths of my being, I truly believe that each one of us needs that special space, however small and insignificant it is to the outsider, where we can be free from public scrutiny. In my work as a writer, which gives me the luxury of working at home, I can afford not to comply with the standards and the expectations of the outside world, with no one telling me how I should look, dress, talk and move. It is a freedom and independence that I crave and cherish. I had worked in the outside world where I had felt strained and chafed against the endless stream of expectations and demands.

Of all people, Sebastien and other children with special needs are in need of this space for their self-esteem. Bombarded by a zillion instructions each day, most of which are not entirely comprehensible, Sebastien needs that space to retreat into himself, if he wants to. Against what people say about autistic people and the need to draw them out from their worlds, I believe that it is equally important to allow them to nestle into the security of their own world at the end of the day. As Sebastien learns to adapt to the demands of the outside world, he needs to feel that he is alright, that there is nothing inherently wrong with him. Whether he is playing in the sanctuary of his room, or tucked snugly within the bosom of his mother's embrace, Sebastien should be given the right to claim that special space of his own—where he is perfect just the way he is.

Meltdowns
(Phoenix, April 2005)

One of the toughest things for me as a mother is to deal with Sebastien's 'meltdowns'. 'Meltdowns'—that is the term my husband uses to describe Sebastien bursting into tears out of the blue, with no seeming provocation. With his lips curled downwards and the profuse tears that run furiously down his cheeks, Sebastien presents a tragic sight. These episodes may last a minute or two, or as long as 30 minutes. At times, they may be accompanied by grunts of anger and frustration, as well as the slamming of his palms on hard surfaces.

It is important to distinguish between Sebastien's 'meltdowns' and the conventional tantrums. While tantrums are dramatic displays designed to get parents to do what the child wants, Sebastien's 'meltdowns' are outpourings of sadness that do not have an ulterior motive. They are challenging for me because nothing I can do can make him feel better when he is going through his 'meltdowns'. Even as he reaches out to me for comfort, my hugs, tender strokes of his swollen cheeks and gentle questioning do not offer any reprieve to him. He only gazes at me with despair, his eyes loaded with the tears about to fall, knowing that he could not convey his feelings and thoughts to me and thus, I could not possibly understand what he was experiencing.

When Sebastien melts down like this, it is often the only way that I know that he experiences profound emotions of sadness, which are often hidden beneath his exterior of silly laughter or seeming nonchalance. These moments often arrive out of the blue—while he watches his favourite television shows that I had taped for him each day ("Barney and Friends", "Teletubbies" and "Mister Rogers' Neighborhood"); after sitting on the swing; after he has been issued too many instructions during homework time.

You can literally watch his gradual descent into his sadness. First, his face begins to crumble into the tragic expression of suppressed tears. Then, his little pitiful face starts contorting in his effort to hold back the torrent of tears that inevitably burst forth, in spite of his best efforts. This is Sebastien at his saddest.

What is even sadder is the fact that I do not know the origins of his sadness. If I cannot figure out the origins of his sadness, then I cannot dig it out from its root, expel it and make it go away—forever. I am so used to coming up with strategies and solutions to resolve his problems that I resent the feeling of utter helplessness and powerlessness.

In the face of numerous meltdowns that have started when he turned four, however, I have had to learn to let go of my need to deal with the problem. I simply let him take my hands to wipe away his tears, hold him and comfort him. Even though I do ask him why he is crying, I know that these questions will yield no comprehensible answers. Still, I mouth these words. I cast them out like fishing nets, hoping to catch something, anything that will give me a clue as to the underlying cause of his grief and anguish.

Upon further reflection, I think that in these moments, Sebastien comes closest to being a typical human being, albeit one who lacks the conventional capacity to articulate his emotions, even though he is experiencing them in a profound way. In the case of typical people, we are able to reach out for help and talk to someone about what is troubling us, when we are feeling sad and upset. Being able to talk about our feelings and thoughts is something that many of us take for granted. One can only begin to imagine the loneliness of an autistic child who has gone through years of being unable to share his feelings of sadness, or even his happiness.

In Sebastien's case, there can be no sharing through words, no real venting of his emotions, except for his occasional outbursts of tears and spurts of aggression, when he just cannot take the world any longer. Unaccompanied by verbal renditions, they have no meaning for anyone else, except for him. So thus, he remains in his lonely world, even as he reaches out. These days, as I watch him cry and seek to comfort him with my useless words that have no meaning to him, I am acutely aware of how he must be the loneliest person on the planet, with all his fears, anxieties and sadness all trapped within him. For him, there is no relief. No one can provide him with any relief from the complex emotions that are plaguing him because he cannot speak about them.

What would I give to have Sebastien divulge the source of his grief during these moments? In the void, I am left to speculate about the reasons for his tears and their relationship to his growing understanding of the outside world, people around him and his difference from them. Is he crying because he notices his inadequacies—his inability to speak or sing Barney songs without hesitation? Is he sad because he looks at typical children with envy, resentment and sadness? Is his grief related to his realisation that he is always 10 steps behind others? Do these moments of clarity plunge him into a state of despair and make him hate himself?

I do not know the answers to any of these questions. I cannot even decide whether I should be elated at his increasing awareness, or distressed by his despair. In the meantime, I try to deal with these 'meltdowns' as best as I can with my damage control measures. They range from consoling him and preventing these 'meltdowns' from becoming aggression to just letting him be whenever it is possible.

One morning at a deserted playground, without a single soul in sight, I had the luxury of letting him vent his anger and sadness, without intervening. The playground provided him with the space that was far less limiting than the confines of his room at home. Thus, he could move about and fling his arms wildly without injuring himself. At the same time, I did not have to worry about him inadvertently or intentionally hurting any innocent bystanders because no one else was around. There was no need for me to think about having to physically or cognitively suppress his aggression.

It was a perfect setting for an imperfect situation.

After my futile attempts to divert him from his 'meltdown', I sat aside, at a safe distance, to observe him. A distance safe enough so that I would not be caught in the crossfire of his emotions. I hid behind my imaginary facade of being Sebastien's therapist, whose role was simply to devise strategies, experiment with them and see whether they would produce the desired outcomes. I pretended to be a dispassionate scientist who had no emotional stakes in the outcome, not a mother who was swept away by her emotion of distress.

So that morning, at the empty playground, on the lovely fresh winter morning, I huddled in the safety of my role as Sebastien's 'therapist' and documented his behaviours in my little notebook. The conversion of the scene into the words on paper erected a fortress of sanity that enabled me to ward away my fears and my sadness. The inherent structured quality of words and the process of writing exerted a measure of control over the chaotic emotions simmering within and raging outside of me.

Not too far away, Sebastien wandered around the playground, sobbing and expressing his grief in unintelligible grunts, while occasionally pounding his chest. Finally, he sat down on the sand, pounding his little hands on the soft asphalt surface of the playground as though he needed to vent the anger that was eating him inside. Watching him from a distance, I could almost feel the helplessness within the expression of his anger. No matter what he did to unleash his anger, he could not make things any better, nor did he seem to feel better.

Although it hurt me to see his vulnerable self out there, pounding on the surface, I decided to leave him alone, thus letting go of my automatic need to save my son, who was, after all, an eight-year-old boy. Somehow, during that peaceful morning, I was guided by a calm certainty that I needed to give him that space to vent his emotions. So long as no one else was around in the public space, he could have all the time in the world to unleash his emotions and I had all the time in the world to wait for him. At least that was how I felt on that comforting winter's morning with a refreshing cool breeze stroking against my cheeks.

Without once looking at the watch to mark the passage of time, I watched him vent, while I continued to write. The truth is that many children, including autistic ones, are given little opportunity to vent their emotions when they reach a certain age and they are expected to adhere to social rules and norms. We do not like to see our children upset. In our love and protectiveness for them, we harbour the delusion that we can always protect them from the ugliness of the outside world and preserve their Disneyland-like childhood innocence. Their sadness and tears force us to face the fallacy of our self-delusions.

Even Sebastien who lives in a fairly protective environment, whether at home or back when he went to school, is not spared from the ugliness of the external world. More often than not, he has been the recipient of dirty looks hurled at him and the mean comments directed at him because of his inappropriate social behaviours. When he was younger, he had a flatness of facial affect that seemed to protect him from the dirty looks he received from others when he inadvertently stepped on their toes and got into their way. I had thought that this fortress was the saving grace of this condition. His growing awareness with his improvements over the years, however, has clearly chipped away at this fortress such that it no longer buffers him from his bruising encounters with the outside world.

Eventually, the judgments of people in public and his peers penetrate his consciousness and eat away at him. Unable to protest against them or speak about them, he traps all of these judgments and his resultant feelings within his body, making him sad and/or angry when he cannot stand it any longer. During these moments, all his anguish and anger about the unfair situations that has accumulated over the past few months are unleashed.

For example, I could not tell you how many times typical young children had cast Sebastien as the villain when he responded in aggression to their taunts and hogging of playground equipment or space. These children, some far younger than him, would then run out to tell their one-sided accounts to their parents, pointing at him as though he were a monster. It used to make me shake with anger to see them take advantage of his silence, his obvious strangeness (for Sebastien's difference did not escape the intuitive and perceptive eyes of children) and his inability to present his side of the story.

While I did not know if Sebastien understood the precise nature of the situation, I was certain that he had a sense that something was not right. Previously, he would have been blissfully oblivious of the human drama swirling around him. At the age of eight, he erupted into tears without being able to explain what was coursing through his mind. It made me wonder how he was making sense of his own disability in a world that acted in ways that were alien to him. I wondered whether he thought about the lack of a niche for him in the mainstream world.

At the end of the day, what these 'meltdowns' do inform me about Sebastien is that just because I am unable to know about the complex causes underlying his grief do not mean that they are not there. So often, we typical people operate under the assumption that the flatness of affect of autistic people means that they do not experience strong emotions. We forget that even typical people who suppress their emotions can cultivate a mask that hides their true feelings inside. Sebastien is not so different from the rest of us, after all.

The big difference is that only he alone can one day discover the answers to the troubles brewing within him because of the lonely planet he inhabits. Much as I wish for an alternative possibility, I know that I can only remain a sympathetic bystander who cannot help him to make sense of his difficult life. I guess a part of my journey is learning how to continue to show my growing child continuous love and support, while slowly letting go of the need to save him.

Grieving
(Phoenix, June 2005)

Recently, I chanced upon an unmarked video of Sebastien and me when he was only 10 months old—the two of us hanging out at the beach in Malibu. This event had long escaped my memory, although it had been captured on video for posterity. My unexpected response to my interrupted viewing of this footage revealed the ever-present process of grieving.

When I saw these images, I felt as though someone had dealt me a hard blow. As I struggled in vain to rise above my sadness and hold back my tears, I tried to distance myself from these two familiar people on the screen. I wanted to observe them as an indifferent bystander who did not know them personally.

This exercise in perspective was not entirely implausible because these two people on the TV screen were intensely familiar, and yet unfamiliar to me, at the same time. Although there was no doubt that I might have known them intimately at some time in our past lives, my travels on the journey of autism had transformed both of them beyond my recognition. The people on the screen no longer bore any connections to our present selves. All that remained was the superficial resemblance in our outward appearances.

Compelling myself to look at the screen, I saw a toddler Sebastien with his puffy infant cheeks and his alert eyes tracking my every move and the ocean undulating in the far distance. His apple round chin was stained red by the juices of the strawberries I had been feeding him. Strawberry is a fruit from which he had turned away for many years. I saw that strawberry-stained face and I wanted to hold onto that image, to return to the time of the taping and to reverse the sequence of events.

And then, I shifted my gaze to the woman—the me almost eight years ago—and watched her unknowing face. A part of me also wished that I could return to being her—the new mother who was getting a kick out of feeding strawberries to her baby, not in the least bit bothered by the juices dribbling down his chin. That was it. The blue sky, the beach with its roaring waves, the redness of the ripe strawberries, an infant and a mother—a paradisiacal world that would bring me to my knees eight years later.

Although I craved to spend more time with that toddler, I stopped the tape and put it away. One day, I will retrieve it and watch it again when I am ready. For now, I lack the courage to do so. My inability to witness these images as an insider has opened my eyes to the grief that I hold in check within me. I could not imagine being the mother who would be confronted with the news of her son's autistic condition only eight months later. Like a time traveller who could see into the future, I could not bear to look at this happy, inexperienced mother who only saw her adorable toddler son with his strawberry-juice-stained chin, without the knowledge of the sadness that lay ahead. Watching her oblivion and innocence, I did not want to be the self-appointed messenger to break the sad news to her, to warn her not to be so happy, because a threatening cloud lay ahead on the not-too-distant horizon.

In reality, of course, I did not have to take on the responsibility of telling anything to this mother. She could be allowed to indulge in her unknowing and enjoy the pleasure of being with her typical son, without the hindsight of what would happen just eight months later. My current knowledge did not make a difference to this irreversible past and what good would this knowledge had done, except to destroy that wonderful day that seemed to have occurred another lifetime ago?

So, I choose not to be the helpless spectator. Not to be thrust back in time into what might have been. Still, my chance encounter with this video footage forced me to realise that I am still, and may always be, a grieving mother. You see, for many years, I had seriously believed that I had conquered my grief. When I spoke to other mothers of children with autism, I had often been struck by the difference between my acceptance of Sebastien and his autism and their sense of sadness or their desire for things to be different for their children.

Crazy as it may seem, I no longer consider Sebastien's autism to be a tragic event, just simply part and parcel of my quirky and challenging life journey. Unlike these mothers, I have not engaged in the periodic exercise of looking back with guilt to see what I could have done differently, try to pinpoint specific events that took place and find answers to what went wrong. In contrast to them, I considered that I was comparatively good at letting go of the 'might-have-beens'.

Prior to the viewing of this video, I thought that I had made peace with Sebastien's condition a long time ago. Essentially, I thought that I had been immensely successful in short-circuiting the grieving process in record time when he was only two and a half years old. It had begun and ended within six months. As I busied myself with trying to help him and dealing with all the associated challenges, there was really little time or energy to wallow in the past and wonder what could have happened. With the passage of time, I learnt to adapt and love Sebastien as he continued to grow and change. As with any mother, I strove to understand him, build on his strengths and cope with his weaknesses.

So what does it all mean—my realisation that I am and always will be grieving? Does it affect how I look at my son the next morning, determine how I feel about my son for the remainder of my life, or make me angry and resentful? The answer is a resounding 'No'. My acknowledgement of the existence of my grief does not enfeeble me, nor alter my profound affection for my son. It simply permits me to experience the emotion that I had denied myself in the past years because I was fearful that my grief would somehow undercut my love for him.

As I discovered through this encounter, I can grieve for the typical toddler son who never grew up, without infringing on my enduring love for Sebastien. Although they are one and the same, these two 'images' of him are entirely different. In the same way, I am no longer the innocent and unknowing mother in the video who could never foresee that one day, she would become a mother who would survive the heartbreaks and emotional turmoil of raising an autistic child and live to tell the tale.

For giving me this opportunity to grieve my loss, I will always cherish this video and the images of our past selves. They offer a baseline comparison to the hard road that Sebastien and I have travelled together. We have done well, in spite of all the sadness and shattered dreams.

Maybe, one day, I will have the courage to put on the video, watch the mother and son, without feeling the need to hold back those tears.

Image of an Autistic Child
(Phoenix, May 2005)

Unlike many parents of autistic children who are embarrassed and/or angry when their children's condition is revealed in the public space, I have no problems with these encounters. As far as I am concerned, it saves me the trouble of having to explain why Sebastien is the way he is when these strangers want to talk to him. When Sebastien and I go out together, I am neither ashamed, nor embarrassed by the fact that he is autistic. In fact, I am proud to declare that I am the parent of an autistic child. There is no shame in this declaration.

So what is the image of an autistic child? Even with one child like Sebastien, there could be multiple facades, depending on how he is feeling that day and the settings. On most days, when he is at a familiar playground, engaged in climbing up the staircase and going down the slides, Sebastien can easily camouflage himself among the other children who are also busy doing the same things. In other instances, his incessant covering of his ears, or the strange hum that emits from his mouth, betrays his 'strangeness' to those who do not know anything about autism. In confined settings such as a doctor's waiting room, when Sebastien used to flit from place to place, without being able to sit down for a second, others would notice something slightly amiss. Others might just hurl me dirty looks that convey their perception of me as a bad mother who had failed to bring up her son appropriately.

As Sebastien grows older, some of his behaviours have become increasingly evident to others that something is not right with him. At that point, the youth of the child is no longer available as an excuse to explain away the weirdness of some of his mannerisms. While this fact of life was hard to stomach at first, I have learned to make peace with the fact that many people perceive my son to be a strange child with weird mannerisms. When they do ask, I simply inform them that my son is autistic. It is a fact of which I am not ashamed.

What does upset me about the outsiders' image of an autistic child, however, is their tendency to view Sebastien through a deficit lens. This deficit paradigm is often used by members of the public to perceive people with special needs; in other words, all that they are thinking of is—'What is wrong with this person?'

Even more disappointing is the fact that this perception is especially cultivated by agencies and professionals whose primary function, whose reason for being, is to provide the necessary assistance to these children and their families. While I was living in the US, I was astounded by the fact that the relevant governmental agencies that funded services there were not interested in what Sebastien could do; rather, their entire focus was on what he could not do. Representatives from these agencies were essentially expected to reduce their autistic clients into a bundle of deficits that could be slotted into different categories—daily living, social, communication, etc.

In Arizona, the Department of Developmental Disabilities (DDD) actually assesses whether and how much autistic children receive in terms of funding to cover all services such as health care and therapy based on an assessment of the deficits. Based on its point system, the more disabled the child is, the higher the score, the greater the likelihood that the families would receive funding and the higher the funding received.

Because of this point system, savvy parents know that they have to present their children as completely inept individuals, lest their actual portrait of their children, regardless of the existence of their developmental disability, renders them ineligible for any funding at all. Essentially, as parents, we must paint our children in a negative light in order to obtain the necessary assistance to help them. We are forced to view them within the deficit paradigm.

So what is the big deal about the deficit paradigm? Parents in Singapore will say that at least the governmental agencies in the US are willing to offer funding to families. Although the funding is wonderful and much needed, the point system that is couched in the deficit paradigm exerts an adverse psychological impact on how parents regard their children with developmental disabilities. In my opinion, people who have conceived this deficit paradigm clearly have no clue as to our struggles with raising our children, or even life itself.

Although we do not delude ourselves about what our children are able to do, we do have to go out of our way to get past their glaring deficits in order to discover their strengths and celebrate their triumphs. To keep going and trudging on this challenging journey, we have learnt to look at our children with a different set of eyes—a perspective that differs radically from those of the members of the public and these service providers. For us to keep going, we cannot afford to depress ourselves by solely dwelling on our children's deficits and difficulties. The last thing they need, and the last thing we need, is a reminder of what they cannot do.

Thus, it honestly makes me wonder how these agencies and the professionals who operate them according to this deficit paradigm can genuinely help our children and help us to help our children. While they offer much-needed money, they chip away at our own dwindling and precious morale. Is that the price that we have to pay in order to get the necessary services we want? Is that why parents and service providers are always fighting over the types of services provided? Either because the services proffered are inadequate, and/or even sometimes irrelevant and inappropriate. What kind of assistance is truly being rendered here?

I think what we parents need more than anything is a sense of hope, a morale-booster, to help us believe that what we do in our day-to-day lives: our busy-ness, our sacrifices, our heartaches and our tears, will make a difference in the lives of our children—that they would not have been in a better place at this point in time had we not made that extra special effort to care for them, to teach them new things in the way that they could understand, to love them and understand them the best that we can. Not because we are trying to impress the outside world, not because we are trying to win the 'Parents of the Year' award, but because our children are our lives. How they are and what they are able to do are a partial reflection of what we, as parents, have tried to do. To put our children down and paint them in a negative light is to devalue the quality of our work and our effort.

All we are asking for from these service providers is to not have to parade our children's deficits in exchange for money. It is like selling out our children and our souls. What we need for these governmental agencies and service providers to do is to support us in all ways by providing the material and the psychological support to enable us to capitalise on the strengths of our children and build on the work that we have already done.

So what is a fair image of a child with autism? Even with the same child, it will differ from person to person, moment to moment, perspective to perspective. All I know is that the deficit paradigm that solely illuminates the deficits of those in our society with special needs do not do full justice to them or to those who love them and know them more than anyone else in the world. Even more importantly, it reflects poorly on a society that adopts a myopic perspective towards individuals and lacks the compassion that characterises the best of humanity.

By being brought up to conform to the rules and norms of society, we often err in our inability to exhibit tolerance for diversity and difference. We glare, criticise and jump to conclusions before we seek to understand. I do not know for sure whether it is the result of socialisation or an inherent human impulse. All I know is that we take away some good away from this world when we, the representatives of the typical population, do not live our lives with compassion.

Believe me, there are times when I wonder whether I too, am imposing the unfair standards and expectation of society on Sebastien when I set the standards high. For example, I do not know whether I am demonstrating the same insensitivity towards him when I try to shape his behaviour so that he is more acceptable to the public eye. Such is the challenge of raising a child with autism for which the price of the ticket for participating in society can be much higher than for the average person. For it involves asking them to play by the rules that are not natural for them, which are created by people who do not think, feel or act the same way that they do. Because Sebastien and others like him are woefully outnumbered by their typical counterparts, they have no choice but to pay the price for the ticket, or else be forever excluded in a realm of their own.

Whether we like it or not, we parents become the manipulators of the fate of our children, as we play the instrumental role in moulding their image—one that belies what is actually going on beneath the surface. This fact is what I fear as I am compelled to take on the decision-making responsibilities on behalf of Sebastien, as though I always know what is best for him, as though I can always make the decision that is in his best interests of my child.

In the challenging task of maintaining the delicate balance between the expectations of the public space and the private world of an autistic existence, I am an arbitrator, deciding how much of the concerns of each world should prevail at each particular moment. When can Sebastien be allowed to act in the way that he wants to? Which settings? To what extent? What will be the consequence of each decision I take? These are all the questions that automatically spring up in my mind as I make these snappy decisions, though the task has become both easier and more difficult over the years.

Thus, the burden falls upon us, the typical parents who straddle the two boats. We are the ones who understand the norms of society, while serving as the representatives of our children and their unique interests. Since it is an uncharted terrain, each of us must draw our own map and find our own path as to how we want to construct the image of our autistic child. Should we embark on a quest to make society accept autistic children, and force society to reshape its perceptions? Or do we try to reshape our child, essentially creating an image that is pleasing to the public, without knowing the exact costs we are exacting from the spirit of our children?

Although there are no black-and-white answers to these questions, I still believe that to be true representatives of our children, we parents must learn to combat against the stereotypical image of an autistic child held by many professionals and organisations within mainstream society. Even as we straddle the two boats as both representatives of our children and as typical individuals, we parents must be able to help our children to transcend these limiting images and enable them to realise their full potential.

Striving for Normalcy
(Phoenix, June 2005)
If there is one primary goal that preoccupies many parents of autistic children, it is that one day, their children will become normal, or

like everyone else in the mainstream society. Considering the fact that many typical people strive to be different from everyone else by being extraordinary, it is ironic that all we parents of autistic children want for them is to be 'typical' or 'ordinary'.

As a typical person who has met many unimpressive typical counterparts, I cannot help, but wonder if 'normalcy' is a commodity that has been seriously overrated by the community of parents with autistic children. In my opinion, our obsession with striving for normalcy for our children fundamentally determines how we feel about them and their future.

Over the years, as Sebastien grows older, it has gotten harder and harder for us to move around in the public space, without his condition escaping notice. His squeals, leaps and hyperactive darts from place to place without thinking of potential collisions with passers-by could no longer 'pass' as the behaviour of a young child when he was eight years old. What was even more conspicuous was his continuous inability to respond to simple greetings and comments from friendly waitresses in restaurants, even though he had acquired the skills to read and write.

Thus, we often attract unwanted attention, annoyed glances and bewildered gazes. I guess it is the typical human response to something that falls out of the realm of the 'normal'. In Sebastien's case, I also notice that I am often included in the stare of disapproval. Because autistic children do not display any obvious differences from their peers in terms of their appearances, many people automatically assume that he is just a poorly-raised child. These looks of disapproval illuminate how quickly human beings tend to judge others in a negative light, without attempting to look at the situation from another perspective, of putting themselves in others' shoes.

Although I do crack down on Sebastien's aggression and other types of behaviours that may cause any discomfort to the outsiders, I give some leeway to some of his more innocuous, but yet strange-looking mannerisms, such as his emission of infantile sounds in the outdoors and his hand-flapping when he was excited in the past. To reprimand him for all of these social behaviours is to deny the existence of his condition and pretend that it is not there. It is like asking a man with an amputated limb to walk on two legs.

At the same time, it begs the question of why some types of socially inappropriate behaviours such as public drunkenness are condoned, or at least more tolerated than those associated with disabilities? Why are we, as a society, so terrified when we are confronted with their unusual aspect?

I cast my judgment on society, not as though I am separate from it. Rather, I consider myself to be a part of the 'we'. If I dig hard enough, I realise that I am often impatient with Sebastien when I am absorbed in my own concerns and priorities for him. It requires tremendous self-awareness on my part to step back and remember his challenges and his attempts to survive and compensate for his deficits. For example, when he still could not differentiate between addition and subtraction at the age of eight, I was overwhelmed with frustration. In my frustration at my fruitless attempts to teach him something that I considered to be very basic, I had forgotten how difficult abstract concepts such as addition and subtraction pose for him. Although I do not think about 'normalising' him obsessively in general, it does come out when I am unable to make any headway with him in specific areas.

As I look at the achievements of people with autism, however,— particularly those who have done so well in life that they are featured in books, articles and television shows, I increasingly wonder: What is the point of striving to make our autistic child act 'normal' as though the objective of 'normalcy' is the only ideal state for human beings to achieve?

Dr Dawn Prince-Hughes, a scientist with Aspergers' Syndrome, challenged that perspective on the 'Jane Pauley' talk show with the observation that in lieu of focusing on the dysfunctionalities of individuals with autism who are often overwhelmed by their surroundings, we should be looking at the world we live in— a world that is filled with toxic levels of noise, sights and sounds. Just because the typical, 'normal' human beings are able to adapt to this environment does not make it a good or healthy environment.

Watching Dr Prince-Hughes on television, I was struck by her extraordinary insights into humanity and the human condition even though she suffers from a condition that makes her feel estranged from the rest of humanity. Through her pain and suffering, she has arrived at a level of consciousness and understanding, which far supersede most typical human beings who do not suffer from any conditions—the 'normal' human beings. Living on the fringe of human life has made her an acute observer and participant of life. Who should be the one to judge who is having the better life, at the end of the day?

Of course, it is evident that not all individuals with the autistic disorder will end up like Prince-Hughes and other well-known figures such as Dr Temple Grandin (said to be the most accomplished adult with autism in the world). I am also not advocating for our children to be left to the mercy of their condition. What I am questioning is this quest for our children to be like the others—the typical children—to be normal, conforming to the norm. Why do we, parents of autistic children, strive only for our children to accommodate a world that often forces people, typical or atypical, to make far too many compromises and sacrifice their individuality and dreams? It truly makes me wonder whether God has created people like Sebastien so that they can challenge the dysfunctional world and reflect back its distorted values and the falseness of its norms to itself.

On these days when I have the luxury of looking at Sebastien, as he is caught up with moving his markers in the air as though they form an imaginary roller coaster hurtling through the invisible tracks, his attention rapt and his eyes focused completely on those markers, I think to myself: "What is really wrong with this picture, even if he does look strange to my typical eyes?" You can say that he is playing inappropriately with the markers, you can take them away and say that he should put them away immediately after colouring with them. Me, I just let him play with the markers because there have got to be a space and time for him to be who he is.

Ultimately, parents who only want their autistic children to be normal often lose sight of the extraordinary gifts, talents and perspectives of their autistic children—the things that typical people do not possess. In their pursuit of the illusion of 'normalcy' as the ideal, they shortchange their children because their children's gifts and talents are unnoticed or unappreciated by mainstream society. So, normalcy is the last thing I would wish for my son. Rather, I want him to grow up to be his own unique being, with his distinctive limitations and his strengths.

Chapter Four
The Healing Touch
(Singapore, February 2006)

Just one month prior to my return to Singapore from the US, I fantasised about the idea that Eastern medicine or treatments such as acupuncture, acupressure or even Chinese herbs, could help Sebastien in the way that Western medicine had not. In fact, at the time of my departure, parents of autistic children in Phoenix, Arizona, were forming a study group to learn and practice alternative approaches and strategies in a book entitled *Energy Medicine*.

My futile search for this book led to me to another life-transforming book that is unrelated to autism—Caroline Myss' *Anatomy of the Spirit*. This book further verified my intuitive sense that I needed to adopt a more holistic and integrated perspective of Sebastien's condition. Instead of viewing his condition as a neurological disorder with its concomitant effects on his body and his mind, I needed to take into consideration the more complex three-way interaction of his body, mind and spirit. Moreover, I was intrigued by her belief that love and harmony lay at the heart of the physical, mental and psychological well-being of all of us and our relationships with one another.

In spite of my newfound sense of interest in this type of thinking, I, who was brought up to be skeptical of this type of philosophies, was clueless about how to proceed with my new understanding of health and its implications for Sebastien. Fortunately for me and him, through a fortuitous series of circumstances, I had the occasion to meet people who would introduce me to two different practitioners of alternative medicine. Both Roger Curtis and Marcio Ribeiro adhere to Myss' philosophy in both their work and how they live their lives.

Roger is a healing massage therapist who utilises a wide repertoire of healing massage therapies that include acupressure and the Hawaiian Lomi Lomi massage. Based on the Hawaiian

Huna philosophy that the well-being of individuals depend on love and harmony, the Lomi Lomi massage involves the use of gentle flowing wave-like movements along the body in order to release body tensions and blockages, thus facilitating the energy flow within the body. Apart from healing their clients with a gentle touch, a Lomi Lomi massage therapist is also expected to do the massage with a complete focus on loving and caring for the client (for more information, please refer to *www.huna.org*).

Watching Roger interact with Sebastien through a series of broad, flowing movements over his body during our first two sessions, I was moved to tears. Never in all my previous years of interacting with professionals had I seen anyone treat Sebastien with so much love, tenderness and respect. At no point during the massage was Sebastien forced or made to shift his body or move against his will. Rather, Roger coaxed him into cooperation by moving his body so gently and slowly to allow him to respond, of his own free will, to some of the movements. If he indicated that he was resistant, Roger simply moved to a different part of the body. At other times, he actually directed Roger to certain parts of his body after experiencing the calming effects. Although he was prone to giggles, he ultimately succumbed to the hypnotic flow of the massage and quietened down considerably as he slipped into a complete state of relaxation and tranquility. True to the philosophy of the Lomi Lomi massage, Roger demonstrated to me the healing power of this gentle touch that was conveyed in a spirit of love.

As I sat in the room, awestruck by this spectacle, with tears running down my face, I was filled with gladness that for the first time in his life, Sebastien was receiving the love and respect that he deserved. During the second session, when Roger turned to me towards the end of his massage of Sebastien, to thank me for the experience of massaging Sebastien, I felt blessed beyond belief.

This was the first time in my life that a professional had thanked me for the opportunity to work with Sebastien. It was always the other way round. Moreover, I often felt bad or embarrassed about some of Sebastien's behaviours or actions that I often considered their work with him to be an imposition for them. In thanking me for Sebastien, as though I had just given him a special gift. Roger highlighted the uniqueness and the value of Sebastien to me. What made it even more special was to know that even an outsider—someone who does not have an autistic child—could appreciate and embrace Sebastien with unconditional love and affection.

After Roger left Singapore to return to Australia, the healing work was continued by Marcio who was a BodyTalk practitioner. Developed by Dr John Veltheim in 1995, BodyTalk is premised on the belief that our bodies possess the innate wisdom to activate the healing process. Regular exposure to daily stresses, traumatic events and environmental factors, however, can undermine the body's healing response due to the breakdown in communication between the different body parts. Through the use of light touches on specific body parts and light tapping on the heart, the practitioner works with the client to restore the flow of energy and the communication among the body parts (for more information on BodyTalk, please refer to the website *www.bodytalksystem.com*).

Although Marcio utilised a different approach from Roger, he shared the same love and respect for Sebastien as Roger had. Highly responsive to Sebastien's movements and non-verbal directions, Marcio worked with and around Sebastien's indications of his preferences and dislikes during the sessions. By earning Sebastien's trust and respect, Marcio was also able to coax Sebastien to work with him in the healing process.

I cannot reiterate the significance of the non-traumatising qualities of these experiences. For Sebastien and other autistic children I know, encounters with practitioners that involve physical contact are often considered to be invasive, threatening and thus, traumatic. Because they are unable to understand what is going on with regard to specific treatments such as a visit to the dentist's office, autistic children often react with a flight-and-fight response to new situations and new people. Insensitive professionals who just want to get their job done will try to deal with the resistant children by overpowering them through the aid of multiple support personnel. While this method had worked with Sebastien when he was young— up to the age of seven—it had very disturbing consequences when he turned eight after he went on and off the GFCF diet. During that period, his aggressive response to these traumatising encounters could go on weeks after the office visit. His body seemed to hold on to his feelings of violation long after the triggering event.

Although I can say that my son is no less autistic than before as a result of these treatments, he has made tremendous strides in the diverse areas of his life, many of which I had previously thought were unattainable. To begin with, he exhibited an extraordinary increase in his attention span that allowed him to focus on his academic work and complete them at double the previous rate. His new-found attention span also enabled him to attend to television and films, which were not possible before. Only after this treatment did I realise why he often misbehaved in movie theatres—because he simply could not focus long enough on the images on the screen to be interested. That was why he, along with many autistic children, could only enjoy a video, after multiple viewings when most children would already have been bored by the experience.

In addition, he showed rapid improvements in his gross motor and fine motor movements. Exulting in his new-found sense of confidence in his body, Sebastien leapt up in the air, ran furiously back and forth across the room with loping strides and jumped up and down the stairs with two feet at the same time—a feat that he could not do prior to the treatment. His fine motor control was clearly enhanced as he exercised tremendous care in wielding his marker to draw the dots in order to create a star, in contrast to his previous efforts that were sloppy by comparison.

This presentation of the improvements in these discrete areas of his life, however, does not do ample justice to the depth and scope of the change wrought within him. How can I put it so that you can fully apprehend my indebtedness to Roger and Marcio? I will try to capture the nuances of the 'transformation' in Sebastien, which is barely discernible to most people.

Because we spend virtually all our waking hours together now that I homeschool him, I am able to discern the tiniest changes in every aspect of Sebastien's being. One of the best things that resulted from this treatment is to be able to really see my son with different eyes, even though I must have looked at him a zillion times over the last nine years. The beautiful eyes that were once marked by their opacity due to the dearth of emotion now brim with curiosity and interest as he gazes playfully into mine, with a smile dancing at the corner of his lips. Even though I still cannot comprehend the message conveyed by his eyes, there is a strong connection between us, which I had never thought was possible before. I had been resigned to the belief that Sebastien, being an autistic individual, would never possess the capacity to reveal the depth and complexity of his emotions outwardly on his face. I could not have been more wrong.

His hands that once knew only how to pull people to get what he wanted or grabbed in frustration and aggression, are now able to caress with gentleness and tenderness. After the first treatment, Sebastien traced his fingers lightly over my eyes, my nose and my mouth for the very first time. The lightness of his touch and his sudden interest in touching my features affirmed my sense that he was also experiencing me for the first time in his life.

Like a blind person who could see for the first time, Sebastien suddenly demonstrated a heightened awareness and interest in his surroundings. Showing detailed attention to many activities, he sought to be involved in the hub of life, wanting to supervise every operation in new settings. Piqued by the world around him, he was no longer as disturbed by experiences in new places as before. Following me on individualised consultations to parents' homes, he seemingly eased himself into each new environment and identified the toys and activities of his interest, without succumbing to his past discomfort and fear of new places and transitions.

During this incredible period, the remaining vestiges of his aggression also faded away as he decided that my opinion of him was important enough for him to refrain from doing something he knew that I abhorred above all else. Just the other day, as I was walking along the typically crowded and noisy CityLink Mall, I realised that I had taken for granted this relatively new feeling of confidence in Sebastien that I had possessed for two months. I was free of my tendency to anticipate when he would unleash his aggression when I least expected it.

Two months ago, even though I had succeeded in managing his aggression fairly successfully, I had not eradicated it completely. Once in a while, such as once a month, when he was overwhelmed by the overpowering sensory stimuli in the environment such as the noisiness and the crush of the crowds in Singapore, he would still resort to aggression.

Not any more...

Far exceeding any of my expectations, Sebastien has turned into a child who can show concern for someone else other than himself. During my interview with Beth, the researcher, two years ago, I told her that I had long accepted that my love for Sebastien could not be dependent on the condition that he could love me back in the same way. I joked that his kind of love smacked of complete utilitarianism: "What can you do for me?" To me, I was easily replaceable so long as someone else came along to satisfy his basic needs.

Today, however, I think very differently about Sebastien and his capacity for love. Although he still demonstrates his love differently from typical people, there is no doubt in my mind that he loves me when he cups my cheeks with his hands during my times of sorrow and gazes into my eyes with a look of concern.

In fact, the 'wonder moments' occur so frequently these days that initially, I experienced an overload of sensations. I needed to do a rapid adjustment to my attitudes and perceptions as I no longer had the energy or the time to bask in my euphoria because to celebrate all the 'wonder moments' would have depleted me. I was a mother who had been accustomed to seeing Sebastien progress at a snail's pace. In the face of these rapid changes, I had a lot of catching up to do.

Throughout these on-and-off-sessions with Marcio, Sebastien underwent a series of powerful purges that were manifested in repetitive and violent sneezes, massive outbreaks of red itchy patches on his body, mild fevers, and most dramatic of all, three episodes of nosebleeds on three consecutive days. It was amazing for me to see how the gentle and light touches of the human body could unleash the toxins that had nestled in Sebastien's body for all of these years. In case you are frightened away by my descriptions of Sebastien's purging process, I want to reassure you that they are only temporary and fade away within a week. Of course, the effects and the symptoms differ from person to person.

Inspired and motivated by their body work on Sebastien, I have also incorporated the massage and Bodywork techniques in my daily repertoire with Sebastien. Using books recommended by them and tapping into my observations of these therapeutic sessions, I have learnt to still my unquiet mind to work on Sebastien's body in a loving way. Although I cannot pretend that my touch has as much healing influences on him as Roger and Marcio, I have experienced the awesome tingling sensation as the energy courses throughout my being in tandem with my movements with him. What I may lack in competence and experience, I more than make up for with my loving hands.

What has been equally important in Sebastien's treatment has been the work that was also done on me. Highlighting the intimate connections between mother and child, both Roger and Marcio recommended that I also undergo their treatments. Whether it was through their healing touches or their willingness to share their philosophies of life with me, I also experienced a significant transformation in my perspective of myself and my perceptions of Sebastien.

Much as I had thought that I had succeeded in loving my son, what I learnt from Roger and Marcio revealed to me that my previous self had not even come close to appreciating Sebastien for the unique person that he was. Overwhelmed by years of struggling to overcome his deficits, I was not even aware of the fact that he might possess certain valuable gifts and talents, which should not be dismissed as 'just an autistic trait'. Now, I see that his attention to minute details allows him to identify distinctive characteristics of things and places far better than typical individuals. He possesses power and strength in his hands that allows him to shape pottery far better than I can. Most importantly, he possesses a strong intuition about people—the gut instinct about which people are kind, which ones are just okay and which ones are simply awful.

In retrospect, I realise that he has always had this uncanny ability about people from the way he tantrummed with certain therapists, session after session, to those with whom he cooperated from Day One. I just thought that his lack of cooperation made life difficult for me, however. These days, I take Sebastien's assessments of people seriously and so far, he has not been wrong. The people he has chosen to enter his life—Marcio and Lay Leng (an assistant who works with Sebastien a couple of times a week)—are all wonderful people with incredible hearts and souls. Therefore, I honestly believe that I have just begun to know my son for who he really is.

With their openness of spirit and their unconditional positive regard for Sebastien—one that is untainted by judgment and comparison with others, these healers treat him and other people with special needs no differently than typical individuals. In their eyes, Sebastien is not a child with deficits; rather, he is simply in need of healing, just as any typical child or adult. Within their therapeutic space, the rigid divide between the typical and the atypical blurs and dissolves away. As Marcio explains it, regardless of our outward manifestations of our abilities, skills, behaviours and appearances (the different coloured coatings of the M&M peanut chocolates), we all share the same core of humanity (the peanut). At the end of the day, I am just as much in need of healing as Sebastien.

So to these two great healing practitioners, I would like to say a big 'Thank You' for the gift of Sebastien. They have given me the faith to see Sebastien as a unique child with tremendous potential and infused me with the belief in his future, whatever it may be.

PICTURES

BEFORE THE ONSET OF AUTISM
—a smiling infant and toddler who loved to pose

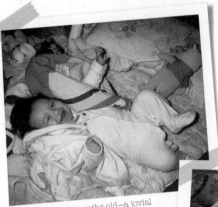

january 1997, 7 months old—a jovial
infant who was always ready to smile
for the camera.

april 1997, 10 months old—
responding to his name
and making normal eye contact.

september 1997, 14 1/2 months old—
still engaged with the outside world, just before
the onset of autism.

ONSET OF AUTISM
—the loss of facial expression and withdrawal into his own world

january 1998, 19 months old—no more smiles for the camera.

april 1998, 22 months old—engaged in repetitive play of putting things into a container.

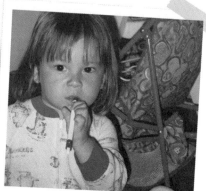

april 1998, 22 months old—needing to place into his mouth various inedible objects.

april 2000, almost 4 years old—occasional smiles again for the camera.

march 2001, almost 5 years old—finally showing affection for 'Doggy', his play companion in social skills training.

february 2002, 5 1/2 years old—wearing a weighted vest to calm him down while playing on the computer.

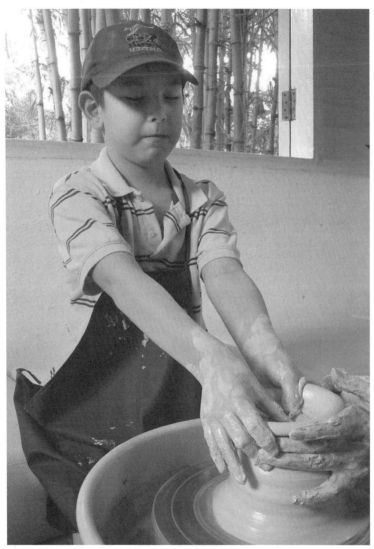

december 2005, 9 years old—enjoying the sensation of clay and the movement of the pottery wheel.

april 2006, 9 years old—riding the cable car for the first time (something unknown that might have frightened him in the past).

may 2006, 9 years old—autographing the picture book about him during the book launch at the Central Lending Library.

Section Two
PRACTICAL SUGGESTIONS

Practical Strategies and Approaches in Raising an Autistic Child

In this section, I have sought to offer a Do-It-Yourself (DIY) approach for educating and raising your autistic child, with a focus on four different areas:

Creating a Dynamic Individualised Home-Based Learning Programme

Dealing with Socially Inappropriate Behaviours

The Role of Alternative Healing Approaches in Achieving Objectivity

Advocacy: The Art of Negotiating with Professionals and Representatives of Educational Institutions and Government Agencies

Because there are many specialists and professionals in the field of autism who have written books and articles on diverse approaches, I have opted to focus on areas in which I could provide parents with original materials and/or perspectives. This does not mean that I have generated these ideas out of a vacuum. Rather, many of these practical suggestions are derived and inspired by existing best practices, although they have been modified and adapted substantially, in accordance with my experience of working with Sebastien.

More specifically, these suggestions are a culmination of my tendencies to adopt approaches and strategies that are truly customised and indvidualised to Sebastien's functioning level, interests and learning styles. In my quest for effective approaches, I have learnt to assimilate, integrate and create new strategies and ideas, which are modified from existing best practices and therapeutic approaches. Through my exposure to these conventional approaches and the assessment of their strengths and weaknesses, I have come to appreciate the value of an integrated, eclectic approach that revolves around a strong understanding of their children.

I want to make it clear, however, that the purpose of this section is not for you to imitate my ideas to the letter. Rather, my objective is to inspire and empower you to create your unique programme and formulate your distinctive approach, which will work for your child. By reading about my work with Sebastien and looking at his work samples, I simply want you to reflect carefully on your child's learning, interests and strengths. Each autistic child is different from another. One learning programme that will work wonders with one autistic child may elicit exactly the opposite results with another. Therefore, feel free to extract what you think is relevant and appropriate for your child and discard the rest.

Ultimately, my aim is to empower you as a parent to take charge of your child's development and education. YOU, not the professionals in your child's life, hold the key to your child's future. At the end of the day, your love for your child, translated into your thoughts, feelings and actions, will constitute the foundation of your child's capacity to rise above his or her limitations to carve a unique imprint in mainstream society.

Chapter Five

Creating a Dynamic Individualised Home-Based Learning Programme

PHILOSOPHY: The Whole Child Approach

The fundamental philosophical tenet of this individualised home-based learning programme is to view your autistic child from a holistic standpoint. Instead of dividing him or her into a series of deficits that need to be addressed separately by different professionals, consider your autistic child as a whole to understand how his or her deficits interact with his or her strengths.

In order to do this, you as a parent, must be willing to suspend your previous conditioning to compare your child with conventional markers and focus on the disparities between your child and his or her typical counterparts. What you need to do is to begin to appreciate your child's uniqueness.

In reality, many autistic children have certain strengths that far exceed their typical peers, even though they may not be traits or qualities that are acknowledged by mainstream society. Nonetheless, the lack of imagination or the limitation of the mainstream society should not negate or devalue the outstanding gifts and talents of autistic children. All over the world, there are autistic adults who are transforming industries and occupations with their unique insights. Therefore, it is important, as parents, that we identify those gifts and strengths in our children and help them to realise their full potential.

Our role is particularly critical in societies, such as Singapore, that value convention and adherence to rules and norms above the assertion of individuality and creativity. Within such controlled contexts, autistic children often fare poorly. Without committed support from parents, they can often fall by the wayside as their gifts are left to languish without inspiration and encouragement from the outside world. Moreover, these children are often made to feel lesser than their typical peers because they cannot perform the conventional learning tasks due to their unique ways of thinking and their challenges.

The creation of a customised and individualised home-based learning programme constitutes the start in your understanding of your child's unique strengths and interests. This will pave the way for your discovery of how to help your child cultivate his or her potential.

DESIGN

In designing an individualised learning programme for your child, I believe it is important to take into consideration two interrelated factors: curriculum and different types of supports.

Curriculum

1. Customise, individualise and contextualise.

One of the chief complaints about autistic children from parents and educators is that they do not like to learn. The truth is that autistic children are often bored by the learning tasks set for them. In other instances, they may not understand the instructions for the learning tasks. As a result, they do not thrive in a learning environment that requires them to do conventional schoolwork because it is often abstract and meaningless to them.

In order to motivate autistic children to engage in learning tasks, it is important to take advantage of their strong obsessions and their adherence to routines and interests. Moreover, their learning styles—many autistic children have a strong visual sense—should be taken into consideration in the design of the curriculum. By recognising the unique qualities and interests of your autistic child, you can create a customised learning programme that is individualised for your child.

Another important selling point of this learning programme is that it is contextualised. By utilising your child's interests and routines and incorporating them into the learning programme, you will make the learning tasks meaningful and interesting because your child can associate them with the world that they know and enjoy.

Guiding Questions:
- What are your child's unique personality traits, sensory issues, learning styles and preferences (see Appendix 1)?
- What are your child's routines?
- What are your child's favourite places?
- What are your child's favourite foods?
- What are your child's favourite activities?
- What are your child's obsessions, passions and interests?
- Knowing the above responses, how do you think they can be converted into learning activities?

These guiding questions are designed to inspire you to think about how you can begin to design your learning activities. The following sections will offer an even more detailed approach in addressing these questions and translating them into action.

2. Mix and match.
As you may know, there are many different types of techniques and strategies for working with autistic children, which have been published by professionals.

Professionals and parents like to adhere to specific types of educational and therapeutic approaches such as Applied Behavioural Analysis (ABA) to the letter. Since I am not an expert in any of these approaches [including Floortime, Sensory Integration, Relationship Development Intervention (RDI), Social Stories, Picture Exchange Communication System (PECS, etc.)] and many books have been written about them, I will not delve into them in detail. I will focus solely on highlighting how I have modified and integrated them to design my learning programme for Sebastien. For more information about some of these approaches, you can refer to my list of recommended books.

In my experience, I have found that an effective approach consists of an integration of strategies and ideas from these best practices. From my perspective and observations, it is not always necessary to follow these strategies to the letter. Rather, you should modify them to suit your child and the environment. Regardless of how widely-used the strategies are and how effective they have been with others, if they do not work after a reasonable period of time, abandon or modify them. This flexibility is essential to the success of your interaction with your child. All autistic children are different from one another. No professional has met every single autistic child in this world to be able to determine what type of learning programme would be appropriate for him or her. You must be willing to be creative in formulating and implementing a learning programme for your child.

Based on this fundamental belief, I have moved beyond the confines of the rules of these best practices to create new strategies and approaches for Sebastien. I call them my 'spin-offs'—creative and novel applications of these approaches—in the creation of my learning activities.

Guiding Questions:
- Which educational and therapeutic approaches do you think work most effectively with your child, based on your understanding of his or her personality, sensory issues, as well as learning styles and preferences?
- Which of these approaches suit your own personality, preferences and styles? For parents who are designing the work, it is imperative that you will be able to invest sufficient time and effort to create the work in the long term. So pick or create something that will feel comfortable, or at least not too foreign, for your disposition.
- How can you incorporate these educational and therapeutic approaches to create and implement an effective curriculum for your child? How do they help you to realise your learning objectives for your child?

For example, I imitated the use of PECS of separating visual symbols and words into individual units by exposing Sebastien to the sequence of words in a sentence. Each word was written in individual word strips without the pictures (as in the case of PECS). Sebastien's quick ability to sequence the words into a sentence without recognising the individual words at the time indicated to me that the breakdown of the sentence into physically separate units helped him to process the information easier than the traditional way of presenting a sentence on paper.

In the beginning, Sebastien viewed these words as pictures by relying on their general shapes and the length of the word to guide him in the initial stages of the reading process. The use of different colours for different types of words to make them stand out from the rest of the sentence was used as additional scaffolding to help him in the beginning (see Sample Learning Activity 1 below).

Sample Learning Activity 1:

In this activity, I asked my son to arrange the individual words that were placed on cut-out strips in the proper sequence. Before doing so, I demonstrated the sequencing of the sentence as I articulated each word slowly. Please note that this sentence referred to a routine activity. Therefore, this sentence was extremely meaningful to him, even though he did not recognise the individual words as yet.

After the demonstration, I prompted him to arrange the word by saying each word at a time and waiting for him to locate the proper word in the sequence. I also provided hand-over-hand assistance when he was unable to locate the word.

| Today | is | Monday | February |

| 1st | I | am | going |

| to | school |

Sample Learning Activity 2:
Social stories that consist of descriptions of places and events, which are accompanied by visual representations such as pictures or photographs, are often used to prepare autistic children for deviations from routines or important events. They typically consist of a description of the background, the sequence of events and directives for action on the part of the child.

At the same time, social stories can be converted into a language learning task to help children to acquire language. In my learning programme for Sebastien, the concept of social stories is translated into the creation of storybooks that deal both with his routines and deviations from them. Supported by photographs or pictures, these home-made storybooks are an effective way to introduce language to an autistic child who can match the language to visual correspondences. The types of visual representation and the level of the language can be modulated in accordance with the unique functioning level of the child.

3. Exercise your creativity and imagination.
Although the prospect of creating a learning programme for your autistic child may seem daunting at first, it really challenges you to tap into your creativity and imagination. Designing a learning programme that will be appropriate and effective for your child requires you to look at a learning task from the perspective of your child and determine whether it will be sufficiently stimulating and motivating for your child.

For example, when you are creating social stories and storybooks, you can decide what type of visual support you want to use. You can utilise photographs taken by yourself or extracted from magazines, draw the pictures on the page yourself, draw pictures on bright-coloured paper which can be cut out and pasted on the page, or even download pictures and photographs from the Internet (see Appendix 4).

Certainly, if your child is high functioning, or extremely interested, encourage his or her initiative in co-creating the storybooks with you. For example, your child may suggest creating a three-dimensional model of a dinosaur park based on your creation of a storybook about dinosaurs (his interest). The creation of the 3-D model can be used to spin off even more storybooks about dinosaurs. So please do not limit your creativity and imagination. Be inspired by your world, activities and the encounter with new media.

4. Utilise a variety of media and presentation formats.

In schools, academic work is typically limited to worksheets that are completed by pen or pencil. For autistic children who have different types of learning preferences and styles, however, plain worksheets can be extremely uninteresting. When they are bored and uninterested, they are not likely to be motivated to engage in the learning tasks.

Based on my work with Sebastien, I can see that the presentation of the learning tasks by utilising a wide variety of media, particularly items from arts and crafts stores, can be very effective in capturing the attention of autistic children. Arts and crafts activities often allow autistic children to explore their learning preferences and work on a wide variety of skills.

For example, pictures made with squeeze tube window paint can be used to create visual representations that are accompanied by a text. Apart from the enjoyable experience of creating a beautiful picture with different colours, autistic children who have difficulties with fine motor control can also work on their fine motor grip and increase their ability to control the squeeze tube paint (see Appendix 4).

When helping autistic children to improve their handwriting skills, you can utilise a wide variety of tools such as stencils, sandtrays or the magna doodle board. The autistic child can also use finger paint to trace letters or numbers, or even paste tiny beads to mark the contours of the letters or numbers. These diverse ways of exposing children to the handwriting experience will increase their interest in this activity.

To bolster the chances of success of your curriculum, it is vital to incorporate various types of supports in your learning programme.

Types of Support

1. Establish expectations and rules of the 'game'.

Because of their feelings of powerlessness, autistic children like the predictability of routines. Therefore, when introducing a new learning activity, you have to be sensitive to your child's aversion to anything new. In the beginning, it is vital that you set up the expectations and ensure that *your child understands* the new rules of the 'game'. I italicise the phrase because we often assume that just because we have explained the rules, our children should understand them. This assumption can lead to tremendous frustration for us and our children. Especially in the case of a non-verbal child with limited language skills and social understanding, it is erroneous to make such an assumption.

Apart from using visual representations to support your verbal instructions, it is important to implement the task and practise the rules consistently to ensure that your child actually understands your instructions. Very often, autistic children fail to perform the task because they do not know what is expected of them. The resultant frustration and the feeling of 'not good enough' can lead to negative behaviours such as tantrums or aggression. These responses are not necessarily a reflection of your child's lack of interest in learning, but your failure to convey your expectations successfully.

2. Use a picture schedule or any type of aids to guide your child in the participation of the learning programme.

Autistic children are known to be highly visual (versus aural). Therefore, the use of a picture schedule to delineate expectations and the sequence of learning activities is extremely helpful for supplementing conventional verbal communication. The picture schedule essentially informs the child about what activities he or she will have to perform—the sequence of the activities and the accompanying breaks.

This knowledge enables your autistic child to have greater control over his or her life and offers a measure of predictability. Allowing your child to have power and control is particularly critical during the introduction of the learning programme. Please note that aids and tools like these can be faded out over time. For example, Sebastien no longer needs these tools because he enjoys his learning activities and responds very well to verbal prompts.

Guiding Questions:
- Does your child require visual support and/or verbal prompts?
- What type of activities do you want to include in your picture schedule? How detailed does your picture schedule need to be?
- All these factors are dependent on the unique preferences and functioning level of your child.

3. Predetermine how structured you want your learning time to be. Depending on the functioning, the learning preferences and the attention span of your child, you need to predetermine how you want to define the learning period.

Guiding questions:
- Do you expect your child to work nonstop for the entire work period—say, three hours?
- Do you want to include breaks that serve as rewards to help him or her stay motivated?
- In my opinion, breaks can not only be a motivating factor, but also something that can contribute to the enhancement of the attention span of the child. The opportunity for your child to get up from a sitting position to move around can be important for stimulating his or her mind. You can use this opportunity to massage key pressure points of your child's body or perform sensory integration activities to exert a calming and relaxing influence on your child.

4. Consider various options and settings for your child to participate in the learning activities.
Although children in the traditional classroom setting are expected to sit at the table to do their work, this work position may be difficult for your child with autism. For unreceptive children who have had negative learning experiences, sitting at a table may trigger task avoidance behaviours and resistance. Once again, taking into consideration the different sensory needs and learning preferences of your child will influence how you choose to design your learning set-up.

Guiding Questions:
- Where does your child prefer to engage in interactive activities, including learning? At the table? On the floor?
- In what position does your child like to learn? Sitting down? Standing up?
- What type of furniture can you use? Can your child sit on an ordinary chair? Or can you use other types such as a peanut ball that will give your child sensory input as he or she sits down?
- In what type of setting does your child learn best? With minimal distractions? With some soft music in the background? With soft lighting? With no pictures on the walls?

IMPLEMENTATION: The Golden Rules of Interacting with Autistic Children in Learning Situations

Speak slowly and quietly to the children in a rhythmic fashion.
Contrary to the human tendency to speak loudly to people who have difficulties in understanding language, educators working with autistic children should speak slowly and quietly to them. This mode of speaking allows the child to process the information without excessive distraction and unwarranted stress and stimulation.

Slowing down the pace of one's speech should also be accompanied by an exaggeration of speech—each word must be articulated slowly so that the child can see the movement of your lips and hear the sounds that are made.

The use of rhythm in speech with a recurrent phrase (that sounds like a chant) can also help to reinforce understanding. Some parents even report the effectiveness of singing instructions to their autistic children and eliciting a far greater response from them than conventional talking.

Repeat yourself as though you were a broken tape recorder.
The inability to understand directions and instructions is a key reason why autistic children fail to do well in an educational setting. Sometimes, it is not because they do not know how to perform a task. They may not understand what is required of them.

The repetition of speech is a key technique in helping autistic children to understand what is required of them or master a task. The act of repetition facilitates the processing of the information for the child. Since many lower-functioning autistic children have information processing difficulties, the repetition allows them to catch more of the information that may have bypassed them the previous time. Even if your child will not be able to understand the full extent of the message the first time, you are one step closer to helping him or her to achieve the desired outcome in the long run.

Limit the repetition to no more than four times—if your child still does not get it, let him or her be. You are planting the seeds of future success. It will happen. Though it may seem discouraging in the beginning, know that you have to start somewhere. In time, your child will grasp the instructions, the word, or the task. You just need to be patient and persistent.

Issue simple instructions.

For non-verbal children or children with limited language skills, issue simple instructions. The number of words should match the number of words actually spoken by your child spontaneously. A child often has difficulties with understanding verbal language because of the time he or she takes to process the message. A five-word message for a child with only two-word spontaneous utterances will be difficult for him or her.

Break things down into discrete steps.

When initiating a new task, look at the number of steps that need to be implemented in order to achieve the final goal. This technique can be used to teach a wide variety of tasks: toileting, academic learning and dressing.

Within an academic context, it is vital for parents to break down what may appear to be a one-step learning task into even smaller steps that can be accomplished by their child with a little assistance and guidance from the parents. Once the child has accomplished the first step, move onto the next. Over time, the child will succeed in completing what may have looked like a highly complex task with minimal stress and maximal understanding.

Practise the three-step hierarchy of interacting with autistic children.

Step 1: Verbal Instruction
Issue a simple verbal instruction to prompt the child to perform the task.

Step 2: Modelling
Demonstrate how you want the child to perform the task.

Step 3: Physical Guidance
Issue a simple verbal instruction to prompt the child to perform the task.

Autistic children, especially those who have limited speech, are particularly disempowered. Adults who interact with non-verbal autistic children often invade the latter's need for physical space and boundaries by physically moving them and directing them immediately (Step 3). These violations include holding onto the children's hand to help them to write without ever letting go, or wrapping their arms around the children's waist to make sure that they are sitting down during 'circle time'. This type of physical guidance can often trigger aggression by failing to respect the children's need for space to move, to breathe and manoeuvre. Typical individuals would also be stifled by this type of physical restraint.

Although the three-step hierarchy should be followed in the aforementioned sequence, it should be related to the level of the functioning of the child. Moderate to high-functioning autistic children typically possess fairly strong language skills and will understand verbal instructions and/or the concept of imitation, and they will most likely respond to the first two steps, without needing the third step. On the other hand, lower-functioning children who have no or limited language skills are not as likely to understand the verbal instructions as their higher-functioning counterparts. Furthermore, being extremely preoccupied with their own worlds, they often do not pay attention to other people and interactions.In this case, these children should be exposed to all three steps in the proper sequence. Doing all three steps keeps open the possibility that the lower-functioning children may now be able to grasp some verbal instructions, without the need for subsequent steps. The important thing is for parents and caregivers to resist the temptation to take the shortcut by physically manipulating their unresponsive children right away, except in an emergency situation, of course.

Finally, it is important to give sufficient pause after each step of the instructions to allow the child to have the opportunity to process the information. In other words, give the child a real chance to demonstrate his or her understanding of the instructions.

Criticise minimally and be generous with your praise and enthusiasm.

Because of their lack of social awareness and other deficits, autistic children often engage in behaviours that require redirection. In other words, they are constantly being corrected. It is equivalent to someone feeling that he can never do anything right, which is very detrimental to one's self-esteem.

Therefore, when correcting your child, explain what he or she is doing wrong, show him or her the right way and leave it at that. Do not dwell on the mistakes, as it will only discourage your child from future effort.

On the other hand, when your child does something right, be generous and expressive with praise. The exaggeration of your expression, particularly in the case of non-verbal children, is a powerful means of letting them understand that they have done something right. So applaud, cheer, or even jump up and down. These exaggerated expressions of emotions are crucial for autistic children, some of who have difficulties with interpreting facial emotions.

Furthermore, since your child seldom receives praises, your enthusiasm will also provide a tremendous boost to his or her self-esteem. Therefore, this aspect of your interaction with your child is particularly important for his or her long-term development and well-being.

Distinguish between sensory and behavioural issues.
When a child is acting out, it is important to determine whether it is a sensory or a behavioural issue. In the case of a sensory problem, the child cannot help him- or herself. He or she may be overwhelmed by the environmental stimuli, thus preventing him or her from performing certain tasks or following your instructions. In this instance, you need to identify various aids or strategies, which can be used to alleviate your child's exposure to the stimuli. This may involve modifying the environment of your learning setting.

On the other hand, when your child has deliberately flouted your instructions or is acting out to achieve his or her own objectives, then this is considered to be a behavioural issue. In this instance, a behavioural modification plan that needs to be implemented with 100 per cent consistency should be formulated. Ultimately, the objective of the plan is to prevent your child from thinking that he or she can get away with doing work by engaging in negative behaviours such as tantrums or aggression.

Identify the 'Antecedents-Event-Consequences' sequence.
These three steps constitute the primary framework of a functional behavioural assessment. It is particularly useful for addressing problematic behaviours in a non-blaming way. When autistic children fail to act accordingly, caregivers tend to place the blame on the children. These three steps will help caregivers to learn how to take responsibility for their part in contributing to the negative behaviour and take steps to correct their role in order to facilitate change in their autistic children.

What a functional behavioural assessment does is to identify the triggers that precede the event; identify the problem behaviour; and determine what was done in response to the event or problem behaviour.

ANTECEDENTS: What environmental and human factors contributed to the occurrence of the event?

To identify the antecedents, try to recall what happened before the occurrence of the event. Was there a slight deviation in routine? Was there an unexpected occurrence such as the sound of a vacuum cleaner? The antecedents allow you to figure out why your child may have acted out in a particular fashion.

EVENT: This event is the easiest to identify—it refers to the problem.

CONSEQUENCE: Identifying your response to the event and the outcome of this response is very important in order to assess its effectiveness and its deficiencies. This way, modifications to the current response could be made to improve the effectiveness of your response.

This three-step sequence will also be particularly important in helping you to decide whether your child's behaviour is sensory and/or behavioural. In this analysis, you will need to figure out your child's motivation, the environmental factors and/or your responsibility for creating the behaviour. Based on this assessment, you can then formulate and implement a new game plan to address this behaviour. Essentially, both you and your child will be expected to modify your behaviours and methods of doing things to eliminate the problem behaviour.

Remain objective at all times, particularly when you are angry.
What this rule means is that you do not let your emotions colour your judgment and assessment of the child. This rule is particularly important when you find yourself getting angry. Children feed off your emotions. When they sense your anger, they will also react

accordingly, depending on their ages and their levels of functioning. Being angry also makes it difficult for you to reflect carefully about the situation and come up with effective strategies to deal with the problem. There will be moments when you cannot help feeling frustrated, however. In these instances, close your eyes, take at least 10 deep breaths, or count slowly from one to 10. If none of these measures work to alleviate the situation, remove yourself from the presence of your child, go to your own room and close the door until you can gather your senses. These simple actions can do wonders in halting the momentum of your own negative emotions.

This rule does not mean you should not get excited and express your joy. In fact, when you are excited about your child's achievement, you should go over the top to express your pleasure.

Be flexible.
Always be willing to discard ineffective teaching approaches. Whenever your child experiences difficulties with performing a task, decide whether the task is appropriate. Is it a realistic task for your child, given his or her level of functioning? If it is too hard, then modify the task in accordance with your child's learning style and preferences. The task may need to be broken down into multiple steps. Consider these difficulties as a challenge for you to understand how your child thinks, instead of feeling discouraged. Your endeavour to identify the most effective approach will bring you another step closer to understanding the workings of the child's mind.

Read your child.
A related aspect is your willingness and ability to read your child. What do I mean by 'read your child'? It means being able to assess the state of mind of your child at every instant in order to determine how best to interact with him or her. Honing this ability will help you to be more and more responsive and attentive to your child.

For example, if your child is having a bad day and displaying symptoms of inattention, it is important to reassess the learning programme for the day. Instead of insisting on the completion of the activity, you may need to come up with a new task, give your child a break, or modify the task immediately. Sometimes, your child's mind may be exhausted by learning a new task. In this instant, there is little point to introduce another new task.

Chapter Six
Dealing with Socially Inappropriate Behaviours in the Public Space

PHILOSOPHY: The Five Philosophical Tenets of Thriving in the Public Space

Respect the public space.

If you want your child to participate in the public space, you must work hard to teach him to abide by what you decide to be the minimum standard of behaviour. To me, this minimum standard is equivalent to a reasonable compromise between your child's ability to live up to these expectations and the social norm.

Unlike a classroom setting, the public space is uncontrolled. It is occupied by a wide variety of people, most of whom do not know anything about autistic people. Thus, it is important for the safety and well-being of your child, as well as those concerned, that he adheres as closely as possible to the social norm. It would be unfair of us to expect others to put up with our children's inappropriate behaviours, especially when they affect the comfort and well-being of other people. In the long term, parents' unrealistic expectations about the public's tolerance can ultimately jeopardise the public's willingness to put up with autistic people or those with special needs altogether.

Set realistic expectations.

The above tenet that does place tremendous pressure on autistic children to behave well should be counterbalanced by this second one. What does it mean to set realistic expectations? Parents must modulate their expectations in accordance with their child's functioning level, the specific settings and the associated social rules. Particularly in the beginning, when neither you nor your child has had tremendous experience with going to new places, you should aim for new places where your child is most likely to be successful. A child who is hyperactive and runs around everywhere will be more likely to succeed at a playground he or she has never been before than a church service or a concert performance.

There are certain places that fall under the absolute 'no-no category' for our autistic children. Places such as churches or concert halls are particularly hard for many autistic children. Unless you can be confident that your autistic child can sit quietly and respectfully without emitting strange noises and fidgeting constantly in their seats for at least an hour, you should be considerate enough to the other patrons by attending these events on your own. It is not realistic of you to expect your child to behave appropriately in those situations. Therefore, should you, for any reason, need to attend these events with your child, please be prepared to leave immediately, should your child exhibit early signs of disruptiveness. Make a quick exit to minimise the damage.

For example, I was forced to bring Sebastien to church because one of the rituals, which was a part of my initiation into Catholicism, was held very early in the morning—too early for me to get a babysitter. With no one else to look after him during the morning hour, I made the decision to take him with me. In spite of my best efforts to redirect him both verbally and physically, Sebastien fidgeted in the seat and even laid down in a sleeping position in the aisle when we as a group of initiates, were kneeling to await the blessing of the priest as he came down the aisle. People sitting in the pews were staring at us with mildly disapproving looks.

In that instant, I felt the oppressive weight of the Church environment on us, which was not dissipated by the kindness of the priest who bestowed a blessing on Sebastien as well. While I was embarrassed by Sebastien, I also knew that it would have been unfair of me to expect him to thrive in such a challenging environment for him. Although it would certainly have been a bonus if he had surprised me by acting appropriately, the fact that it did not happen was something that I had anticipated. So, when we finally completed the ritual and left the Church, I did not reprimand him at all. In fact, I simply shrugged off the experience, turned to him and said in my carefree voice: "That was not too fun, was it? Now let's go to the Third Street Promenade (his favourite place)."

This is not to say that as parents, we should not take risks and expect our children to behave well in certain challenging events and places. What I am suggesting is that we as parents must have the right attitude and preparedness. The maxim of 'we hope for the best and prepare for the worst' holds true in how we should approach these high-risk situations.

Stay cool...even when you are shaking with rage inside.
Especially in the public space, your reaction to your child's misbehaviours is very important. Very often, parents' physiological reactions to their children's behaviours can either alleviate or exacerbate the situation. Our children feed off our emotions, especially those with limited language skills. Their lack of verbal communication skills is compensated by their acute sensitivity to our tone of voice and states of mind. So, when we lose our cool and explode in front of children, we may also trigger similar outbursts from them. At this point, both you and your child will be regarded as a nuisance to society.

What is most important in maintaining our objectivity is that it allows us to concentrate on what our children have done and how to deal with the problem in a productive way. Only with this level of calmness will you even remember your great behavioural management plan and be able to implement your strategies consistently. Conversely, if you are caught up in your own feelings of anger, frustration, irritation and even desperation, there is absolutely no way that you will be able to engage in these constructive thought processes.

While the crisis is occurring, you must separate your emotions from your child's actions. During these moments, you must stop feeling like a parent and acting like a therapist.

Listen to your child when he or she is non-compliant and aggressive.
Although these behaviours are unpleasant and you wish that they would not exist, they serve as a powerful form of communication, particularly in the case of autistic children with limited language skills. With their lack of facial affect, these autistic children actually convey the impression that they do not feel anything or care about

any situation, until they erupt. It is only when these moments occur that they capture the attention of their caregivers or educators.

Therefore, even as you adopt a behavioural management approach in eradicating undesirable behaviours, you must also seek to examine the underlying factors that may be contributing to your child's non-compliance and aggression. Essentially, you will need to move beyond the behavioural management approach to determine how you can alleviate the situation by formulating an even more comprehensive strategy to reduce your child's motivation to engage in these negative behaviours. This understanding will also help you to identify strategies that will be effective in eradicating your child's bad behaviours.

For example, if your child's behaviour is attention-seeking, you should examine how you have failed to show him or her adequate attention to decrease the need to seek your attention in the negative way. At the same time, your behavioural management strategy for eradicating the behaviour may involve ignoring it, instead of kicking up a big fuss about it. It is important to point out that the same behaviour with different motivators will need to be dealt with differently.

Believe in your child.
Finally, to expect your child to meet social expectations in the public space, you have to believe that he or she child can make it, if not today, then maybe in a week, in a month, or a year.

APPROACH
In dealing with socially inappropriate behaviours, behavioural management approaches are highly effective in obtaining the desired outcomes. To put it in a nutshell, a behavioural management approach encompasses three components:

Set out the rule and make sure that your child understands it.
In order for your child to be able to comply with your rule and accept it, he or she must first be able understand the rule. This means that you must present your rule in a manner that can be understood by

your child. While autistic children with strong language comprehension may understand verbal explanations easily, others with limited language skills will require a picture such as a PECS icon to support your explanation. You can also dramatise what you mean by acting out the inappropriate or appropriate behaviour, while articulating your rule.

Regardless of the rule, you should be able to incorporate the content into this template:

DO NOT DO (the undesirable behaviour).
If you do it, you will experience (negative consequence).

Conversely, you can also encourage positive behaviour in a similar way:

DO (desirable behaviour).
If you do it, you will be rewarded (positive consequence).

The balance of rewards and punishments is vital to the success of a behavioural management programme.

There are some parents who are very uncomfortable with using rewards and punishments to teach their children. In my opinion, it is a matter of perspective of changing your paradigm about the behavioural management programme. Instead of seeing it as a rewards and punishments system, you should realise that this model is designed to teach our children to take responsibility for their actions. Autistic children who have a limited sense of right and wrong because of their difficulties with understanding social norms, learn to differentiate between what is right and what is wrong, only when they see that certain behaviours elicit a positive outcome and others do not. Thus, they can begin to create a moral map of what is right or wrong.

Your child, however, will truly apprehend the significance of the rule, or consider it to be a rule only if you implement it immediately and consistently.

Implement the rule with 100 per cent consistency.
In short, your child must understand that you mean business with regard to this rule. To achieve this level of consistency on many rules can be extremely difficult and unrealistic. You can, however, hone in on the specific behaviours that are most troubling to you and formulate the 'no-budge rules'. These will be the rules that you must enforce with 100 per cent consistency.

Many parents often abandon this approach when their attempt to implement this behavioural management plan incurs an even more extreme adverse reaction from their children. They quickly assume that this plan does not work for their child.

Nonetheless, if you think about it, you should realise that no one gives up power and control without a fight. Your erratic implementation of the behavioural management plan and giving in to extreme tantrumming will only convince your child that the new way of getting what he or she wants is through extreme tantrumming, with a good percentage of success. The absence of consistency holds out the hope for these children that on a lucky day, they may just get what they want.

You can increase the stakes of the behavioural management programme by using a 'stars' and 'sad faces' system. At the end of the day, your child will face a reckoning before you—the 'judge'. Based on your child's performance with regard to a specific 'no-budge rule', you will decide whether your child deserves a 'sad face' or a 'star' for the day. The accompaniment of the symbols with positive or negative consequences will infuse these abstract symbols with tremendous power.

For high-functioning autistic children who are often motivated by a system of rewards, you can further encourage them by allowing them to convert the stars at the end of each day or each week to tangible rewards.

In Sebastien's case, 'sad faces' that were doled out in response to any episode of aggression, regardless of its severity, was accompanied by the removal of his favourite toys from his room. Conversely, 'stars' were celebrated with a return of these favourite toys. When we came to Singapore and the physical environment was changed, I discovered that he had attached tremendous value to these 'stars' and 'sad faces'. I only need to refer to them to get him to check his behaviour. Even I was astounded by the sheer power of this conditioning process.

Assess the effectiveness of your rule.
The objective of your rule is to eliminate undesirable behaviours. If, however, you have been 100 per cent consistent in enforcing this rule and see no positive changes whatsoever, then it may be time to reflect carefully on the different aspects of your rule. Here are some guiding questions to help you decide the underlying cause of the failure of this rule:

1. Are your expectations realistic for your child, given his or her age and functioning level? In other words, does your child possess the maturity, the ability and/or the skills needed to follow the rule?

2. Do you think that your child understands the rule, that his or her inappropriate actions will lead to the consequence? In other words, have you been 100 per cent consistent in enforcing this rule in a timely fashion? Especially in the case of an autistic child with limited language skills, the delay in meting out the consequence may undermine the association between the event and the consequence. At the end of the day, the child has not really grasped the rule.

3. Is the consequence—the key part of your strategy—something that matters to your child? Whether it is a punishment or a reward, the consequence must be something so significant to your child that it will deter or motivate him or her. In Sebastien's case, I really had to increase the stakes in my struggle against his attraction to the power of aggression. I had to make sure that the consequence was so unpleasant that it made him think twice about offending.

4. Has your child grown and changed his preferences? Essentially, a consequence that could have meant a lot to your child a month ago might have lost its importance now. The decrease in the significance of this consequence will also undermine the effectiveness of your rule. When your child no longer cares about the consequence, his or her motivation to act appropriately may also fade away.

I must point out, however, that when our children act out in the public space, it is also vital to take into consideration the possibility that they cannot help themselves. This issue is particularly important in the case of young autistic children with a delicate neurological system and/or those who exhibit strong sensitivities to environmental stimuli and lack the knowledge and skills to self-regulate.

Between the ages of two and four, Sebastien would break out in tears and tantrums in the public space, without any obvious provocation and desire for anything. Over time, I realised that, with his hypersensitive ears and his inability to visually tune out details in his environment, he could get easily overwhelmed simply by walking on the streets. In such instances, a behavioural management approach would be highly inappropriate.

So, what types of behaviours fall under the category of 'behavioural problems'? Here are some examples:

- When your child throws tantrums after you refuse to buy or give him something in an attempt to get you to change your mind.

- When your child engages in an act of aggression in order to get you to do something.

- When your child refuses to comply with your instructions even though he understands them.

- When your child engages in any form of controlling behaviours such as tantrumming when you change routes and refuse to eat at specific locations.

What these examples of behavioural problems illustrate is that when children seek to utilise tantrums or aggression to get what they want and impose their will on others, you have a behavioural problem.

IMPLEMENTATION: The Five Golden Rules

Do your homework.
Make the necessary preparation for your child to succeed, particularly when you are planning to go to a new place or attend a challenging event. Visual schedules and social stories that offer your child background information and your expectations for the event may be utilised to prepare him or her ahead of time. Knowing what will happen ahead of time will minimise the level of stress and anxiety that your autistic child will experience because most autistic children dislike new and unpredictable places or situations. Their feelings of fear and anxiety are then manifested in tantrums and acts of aggression. I have used social stories successfully to help prepare Sebastien for threatening events such as moving house.

With new and unfamiliar places, you may need to play the part of an investigator to obtain information about the background of the place in order to help you in your preparations. For example, when Sebastien and I were invited by a singer to listen to her band perform at a restaurant in the five-star Fullerton Hotel in Singapore, I went through a series of preparations.

Because I had never been to the hotel or the restaurant, I was only able to discern that it would be a challenging place based on the impressiveness of its external facade. Torn between attending the event on my own or taking Sebastien with me, I decided to resolve the situation by calling the restaurant manager and learning more about the setting.

The conversation went something like this:

> Kah Ying: On a Friday night, are most of the patrons adults or are there families?
> Manager: It is hard to say, but usually, there is a mixture of adults and families.
> Kah Ying: Would you describe your atmosphere as quiet or noisy?
> Manager: Well (he hesitated), it is the usual restaurant noises.

Based on this brief exchange, I concluded that Sebastien did not need to live up to impossible standards such as sitting quietly in his seat because he would be surrounded by well-behaved adults who would be perturbed by his behaviours. Rather, with the presence of other children, there is always a chance that they will not be very well-behaved, thus taking some of the heat away from Sebastien. What was funny was that my line of questioning placed the manager on the defensive. His responses and hesitation indicated that he thought that I was an adult woman who was aiming for a sophisticated dining atmosphere with a male companion. I could almost hear a sigh of relief on his part when I told him I would like to make a reservation for me and my nine-year-old son.

Even though I made the decision to take a risk, it is important to emphasise that I was perfectly prepared to leave the restaurant immediately, should Sebastien prove to be disruptive. To me, going to the restaurant at the Fullerton Hotel was a close second to attending a church mass.

On the night of the performance, I even brought along an electrical massage cushion to provide sensory input to Sebastien and his magna doodle board to occupy him, while we waited for the food. Then I perused the menu carefully and ordered food items that were likely to be eaten by him, although you could never be sure with him. Any aberrations in the presentation of the food could lead to a complete rejection of the food items and the difference between a good or a bad evening.

In the end, Sebastien passed the Fullerton Hotel test with flying colours. With his head tilted sideways to cover his exposed right ear with his shoulder to modulate his exposure to the loudness of the band and the background noise of the environment, Sebastien used his right free hand to draw on his magna doodle board until his food arrived. Then, he was occupied with eating. Although he did not behave in conformity to the social norms in his posture and need to engage in non-dinner activities, he was not disruptive to the dining environment and the evening's atmosphere. In fact, he barely registered a look from many of the restaurant patrons. Prior to attending this event, I did tell my friend that we would leave the premises immediately should Sebastien prove to be disruptive to the performance or the setting. So, after the show, she complimented Sebastien: "You were so good. You can come to the Fullerton anytime." Another 'wonder moment'.

Don't aim for the stars... at least not right away.

Although it is good to have a final goal in mind, I think it is important for parents to start off this process by going for small and realistic objectives. This is not the same as setting low expectations for your child. Rather, you are mapping out a way for your child to be successful by offering him or her the necessary scaffolding to move up to the next level at his or her pace, not yours. The achievement of these smaller objectives will give your child an opportunity to celebrate his or her accomplishments, and allow you to acknowledge the progress that has been made and give yourself a pat.

Dramatise and exaggerate.

When meting out the consequence, help your child to understand how you feel about the behaviour by matching your facial expression and tone of voice to your emotions. Why is this dramatic performance necessary? Its purpose is to enable your child to distinguish between his or her positive actions and negative actions. For autistic children who lack an inherent understanding of social norms and morals, they rely on the reactions of others to help them distinguish between right and wrong. You must operate on the assumption that your child is clueless about which of his or her actions is appropriate and which one is not. Only by providing your child with noticeable feedback can you help him or her to discriminate between them.

In your dramatic representation of your external emotions, strive to capture your child's attention by exaggerating your facial expressions, expressing yourself with your body language by using big gestures and speaking with the right tone of voice. This means that when your child does extremely well, you need to show your pleasure by clapping your hands, flashing a long lingering smile, cheering wildly as you jump up and down. On the other hand, when your child has misbehaved, you should look at him or her sternly and speak in a low tone to express your disappointment or unhappiness, as you deliver the bad news of the undesirable consequence.

Certainly, it is important to match your dramatisation to your child. The more your child is able to recognise you and acknowledge you, the less you have to dramatise yourself. In my interactions with Sebastien, I have decreased the intensity of my dramatisation with his increasing awareness of his surroundings and the people around him. So, even though you may think that dramatising yourself is an extremely tiring process (yes, your jaw will hurt and your body may ache in the early days), know that this situation will not last forever.

Furthermore, you should also modulate your dramatisation in accordance with the momentousness of the event or the seriousness of the 'crime' committed. Your modulation will also help your child to understand gradations, that there are certain poor behaviours that are worse than others and good behaviours that are better than others.

Evolve with your child.
Whatever behavioural management approach you choose to do, you must individualise your approach to the level of your child's

awareness, language skills and understanding of social norms ... at the stage of his or her growth and development. Your child will not stay the same. As your child grows older and makes progress, you must be prepared to modify your methods accordingly.

This process does require a degree of trial and error. When something that used to work very well in conveying your emotions to your child no longer elicits the outcomes as it did in the past, it is time to let go. Parents who struggle to find the winning solutions are often unwilling to relinquish these successful, but obsolete, approaches. They have enjoyed being in the 'cruise control' mode for all this time that they refuse to return to the world of the unknown again—that trial and error phase of formulating the 'winning' solution.

I know about this because I used to be one of those parents who crave to get into the 'cruise control' mode. With Sebastien, the 'no meany face' approach to control his aggression was my 'winner' for the longest time—it reigned for three years. Although it did not eradicate his aggression, it did sufficiently well to impose a degree of control on it.

Sebastien's aggression that was triggered by his response to the GFCF diet, however, took on an entirely different character. With his act of aggression appearing at the same time as the 'no meany face', the former approach was rendered obsolete and useless as a warning sign. I was hurled back into the world of the unknown again in quest for my next 'winner'. I think my efforts in the beginning were rather useless because I clung onto the 'no meany face' approach by spawning alternative expressions such as 'get a grip' when Sebastien began to hum a tune that typically signified his rising agitation.

As you had read in my essay on my efforts to deal with Sebastien's aggression, you would have seen that I had to really think outside of the box to come up with a multi-pronged approach to deal with his aggression which was far more complex and sophisticated. What was evident to me was that it was not possible to treat 'Sebastien, the eight-year-old' with his emerging masculinity and assertion of independence, in the same way as 'Sebastien, the five-year-old'.

Back then, the 'no meany face' approach that was coupled with a big scolding for his 'meany' action was effective in helping him to understand my anger and displeasure. Back then, Sebastien used to laugh at my expression of anger; my scolding strategy was designed to make sure that he did not dismiss my anger as a laughing matter.

At the age of eight, however, when Sebastien had already understood the emotion of anger, scolding him only triggered a violent physiological response and more aggression in him. My previous strategy was thus, backfiring on me. Yet, in my stubborn fashion, I persisted in employing this approach until I read the Redfield book and followed an opposite tack.

So, please learn from my lesson. When a 'winner' does not work anymore, let it go.

Persevere without fear.
Parents with a soft heart are put off by the process of the behavioural management approach. Hating to see their children upset in any way, they start crumbling in the face of their child's howls or protests and cave in when the going gets tough. I have walked into many households where a pint-sized boy with no language skills has succeeded in 'training' all the adults in the household to bow down to his will at the slightest whine and a hand gesture. Some of these loving parents often joked that their children are kings and queens who decide where the family goes for the outings and how long they are able to stay at various places. Essentially, the will and desires of the parents become ruled by their 'helpless children with special needs'.

What these parents forget is that they are not doing their children any favour by giving in to them at all times. Their pint-sized children will not remain pint-sized and cute forever. Without proper guidance and the respect for adults, these pint-sized children will grow up to be tyrannous adults who will expect the whole world to bow down to them or lash out in fury and/or engage in other inappropriate social behaviours.

Through my individualised consultations, I have encountered many loving parents who harbour the notion that their non-verbal three-year-old children should be cut a lot of slack because they are so helpless. Thus, they are surprised when I point out the fact that these helpless three-year-olds must not be so helpless and powerless when they have succeeded in 'training' their parents to follow their every whim without ever uttering a single word. I make a joke that these children are even more impressive than many CEOs that run huge corporations who can train their subordinates to know their wishes with a little grunt and a little whine. Even as they laugh about this metaphor, these parents are also dealing with the shock that they have been 'deceived' by their seemingly helpless children.

For months and years, these children have succeeded in wearing down their parents with their tantrums, pitiful looks, tears and arching backs. To achieve this level of supremacy over their parents, these children have certainly outplayed and outlasted their parents in their ability to carry on their dramatic displays of displeasure. So I say to these parents, it is time to turn the tables on these children and show them that their parents can play this game better than they can. Only when you prove yourself to be a worthy adversary to your child will you ultimately be successful in earning his or her respect. And with respect will come compliance, cooperation and connection.

During one of my recent visits to a mother with a moderate to high-functioning six-year-old autistic child who has strong language skills, she remarked that Sebastien would respond immediately when I issued instructions to him, even though he clearly demonstrated far less language skills than her son. While it is evident that her son has no difficulties understanding what she is saying, he is choosing not to comply with her command 'to come here'. This is a behavioural issue.

Apart from giving her some ideas and strategies, I told her this important truth that should constitute the ultimate outcome of any type of strategy to eradicate socially inappropriate behaviours—respect:

"Sebastien respects me. What I say, think and feel about him matters to him. So, when I ask him to do something, he will do it immediately. But it is a respect that you will have to earn."

Once you have gained your child's respect, you will no longer be solely dependent on your rewards and consequences, 'stars' and 'meany faces'. Your child will want to act well because what you think and feel about them matters to them.

Chapter Seven
Role of Alternative Healing Approaches in Achieving Objectivity

PHILOSOPHY

One of the things that has helped me in my journey of raising Sebastien and enabled me to maintain my sanity is the recognition of the importance of achieving objectivity. What do I mean by objectivity within the context of raising an autistic child?

Objectivity, in this context, is the uncanny ability for us parents to remain calm and collected in the face of eruptions of stressful crises that trigger out-of-control emotions within us.

Many of us parents feel that these crises often arrive at the most inconvenient and inopportune of moments, although in actual reality, there is never a good time for their arrival. These temporary crises may take the form of your autistic child screaming his head off because he had vomited during a rocky boat ride and insists on getting off the boat even though you are still fifteen minutes away from the shore (Yes, it happened to Sebastien and me!). Or you come home after a stressful day at work only to encounter your non-compliant child who has just messed up your immaculately arranged CD collection when you had been so longing to relax to listen to your meditation music. During moments like these, it can really be difficult not to explode and 'lose it'.

Yet, these are precisely the moments when you must hold onto your cool and your sanity. Only when you are in a state of objectivity can you formulate and process your ideas to get yourself out of the situation. You need to have a clear head to not only come up with ideas, but stick through the situation: When Strategy A does not work, you have Strategy B. In fact, this focus on generating ideas can also be extremely helpful in distracting you from a far more tempting, though destructive, course of action—succumbing to your emotions.

Although I have had my fair share of successes, alongside my even more spectacular failures, I have finally discovered the key to achieving this objectivity. You can achieve the stoic demeanor and retain the clarity of your mind without turning into a robot. One of the promises that I hold forth in my parent training programme is to share with the parents my formula for raising an autistic child without getting sucked into the crises that can take away from you the pleasure of this journey.

Unfortunately, for those of you who are waiting for the magic solution and panacea that will fix this issue once and for all, I am sorry to tell you that there is no shortcut. My formula is this: a daily routine of conscious breathing through my diaphragm, acupressure, meditation and the manipulation of energy, also known as *La Qi* (literally translated as 'pull energy') for at least an hour. Each morning, before Sebastien gets up and before we get caught up in doing academic work and participating in mainstream society, I practice my daily routine. Although it may seem like a chore to adhere to this routine at first, I have experienced its power and calming effects. Thus, my persistence to pursue it. Now, it has become an entrenched part of my life.

Since I am not a specialised practitioner of any of these approaches and there are books that have been published on these subject matters, I will present my perspective on two key books that have taught me about acupressure and conscious breathing, as well as describe my experience with a Chinese master who demonstrated the basics of the technique of *La Qi* to me.

Michael Reed Gach, *Acupressure's Potent Points: A Guide to Self-Care for Common Ailments*, New York: Bantam Books, 1990 (ISBN 0-553-34970-8)

Recommended to me by Roger who has learnt how to utilise, modify and combine the information in his application of the acupressure points, Gach's book is a 'must-have' for all households. Accompanied by clear diagrams, photographs and precise instructions on the locations of the specific acupressure points, this book has been invaluable in empowering me to recognise the power of my healing hands and the body's innate potential for healing.

Although I do use this book to help me to deal with common ailments such as colds and flu, headaches and backaches, I was initially drawn to this resource because of its coverage of ailments that are often manifested by autistic children. They are: 'Anxiety and Nervousness', 'Irritability, Frustration, and Dealing with Change', as well as 'Memory and Concentration'.

As many of the parents with autistic children will attest, these three types of difficulties are often experienced by our children. Due to their need to control their environment and their need for predictability, autistic children are easily irritated and frustrated by the prospect of change. Their responses to these situations typically stem from their feelings of anxiety and nervousness. Another primary deficit they face, because they cannot tune out to their surroundings, is their lack of attention span, unless they are doing something that is very interesting to them. In these instances, particularly when they are sitting at the table and doing academic work, parents can actually utilise some of these acupressure techniques on them to enhance their concentration and focus.

At the same time, I also see that the execution of many of these same acupressure points can also be effective for us parents to gain a command of our emotions and experience the feelings of peace during moments of crises. In the early days, I realise that skipping one day can mean the difference between having a good day or a bad day with Sebastien. On my good days, I can handle anything he may throw at me; on a bad day (when I am suffering from premenstrual syndrome and skipped my routine), the slightest things that Sebastien does could set me off and ruin the day for both of us.

Finally, the best selling point about acupressure is its portability. As with wireless Internet access, you can literarily use it anytime and anywhere; but better still, you do not have the inconvenience of having to carry any additional equipment with you. The only equipment you need is your hands. Recently, since my daily routine has been disrupted by the arrival of an abandoned infant kitten we saved, I practice my acupressure strategies while commuting on the MRT, whether I am standing or sitting down. So long as I have a free finger for me to apply firm pressure to the key acupressure points, I am able to summon the feelings of calmness and focus into my being.

Gay Hendricks, Jr., *Conscious Breathing: Breathwork for Health,*
Stress Release, and Personal Mastery, **New York: Bantam Books,**
1995 (ISBN 0-553-37443-5)

Although I never finished reading this book because I got interested
in the acupressure book, I was glad that I learnt the fundamental
technique of conscious breathing—breathing through the diaphragm.
From this book, I learnt that the act of conscious inhalation involves
the conscious coordination of the nose taking in air, the rise of the
chest, the inflation of the belly like a balloon and the accompanying
arching of the back. Conversely, the process of conscious exhalation
encompasses the orchestrated movements of the nose releasing air,
the fall of the chest, the complete collapse of the belly and the thrust
of the back backwards.

What really caught my attention about Hendricks' book was
how something as simple as breathing could make or break our
well-being. Even though I was tempted to skip the part of the book
that enumerated the benefits of breathing in order to get to the
action, I was glad that I bothered to read about it because it served
as a constant reminder of the 'rewards' of conscious breathing.
As pointed out by Dr Hendricks, conscious breathing can decrease
stress and tension; boost physical energy and stamina; enable
one to take control of his or her emotions; enhance our immune
system; alleviate pain; mitigate the decline associated with ageing;
heighten memory and concentration; as well as stimulate an
overall psychological and spiritual transformation.

After reading that list, I was sold! Even more importantly, in my
first encounter with exercising this simple technique of conscious
breathing, I was struck by how something as simple as breathing
could make me feel so rested and tranquil. Furthermore, the
breathing technique was needed for me to fully benefit from the
effects of acupressure. Mr Gach emphasised the need to engage in
deep breathing, while applying firm pressure on the acupressure
points. What he counted on was that people actually knew how to
breathe deeply!

The actual reality is that in the hustle and bustle of daily
stressful living, many of us, especially parents who lead hectic
lives of juggling multiple responsibilities, have forgotten how to

breathe! In fact, when I was showing the parents the technique of conscious breathing, the parents joked that it was bad that they even had to be trained on how to breathe! Thus, it was little wonder that I experienced tremendous difficulties in getting the parents to relax themselves sufficiently to allow their bodies to rise and fall, in tandem with the intake and release of their breath.

Therefore, Dr Hendricks' book is an important precursor to Mr Gach's as we parents have to get down to the basics and learn everything from scratch, including something that we take for granted—breathing. Even more portable than acupressure, the act of conscious breathing is really something that we should be doing every waking moment of our day.

If I have succeeded in getting you excited to learn about these life-changing techniques, please purchase these books to learn how to execute these moves.

La Qi

Before proceeding to talk about this technique, I want to highlight the fact that my sole knowledge of this practice stems from my isolated encounter with a Chinese *Shi Fu* (literally translated as 'Teacher') who was utilising the sheer energy emanating from his hands for healing purposes. From a distance of 30 feet, I could actually feel the palpable heat of his hands, while they hovered over the head of his client. Although I did not know him well, nor did I know much about *La Qi*, I was sufficiently intrigued to seek his knowledge and wisdom about how his technique could be used to help Sebastien with his condition.

Right away, he offered to show me how to do the basic version of the *La Qi* technique and told me that once I could generate the energy with my hands, I would simply need to 'hover' my hands over any part of the body and transmit my healing energy to Sebastien. Basically, his instructions were as follows:

1. With your eyes closed and sitting in an upright, but relaxed posture, make sure that the palms of your hands are facing one another. Then move them towards and away from one another in front of your belly as slowly as possible.

2. At the same time, focus on the empty space between your hands as you move them as close to one another as possible without touching and move them apart.

3. In the process, you will experience rising heat and magnetic energy that will draw your hands together and repel them from one another without any conscious movements on your part.

4. Once you have mastered this technique, you can transfer positive energy to others and transmit positive thoughts and wishes for their healing when you are hovering your hands over their bodies.

Of the three types of alternative healing techniques described here, I encountered the greatest difficulties in learning how to *La Qi*. While I could experience the effects of conscious breathing right away and acupressure techniques to some degree within a few days, it would take approximately two weeks before I would experience a breakthrough in *La Qi*.

Without the support of any written materials, I could only replay the Chinese teacher's verbal instructions over and over again as I executed the physical movements. What I found extremely difficult was the simultaneous need to concentrate on the empty space between my eyes, while being relaxed at the same time. I had thought that those two states of mind were irreconcilable.

Finally, one day, it occurred to me that I needed to allow my shoulders to relax and slump down as I moved my hands in front of my belly. When I was able to relax, I felt a powerful jerking sensation that forced my hands towards one another. When it occurred, I knew exactly what the Chinese teacher meant by magnetic energy. Buoyed by my success, I was tempted to leap up and share the news with my family. I was, however, immediately conscious of an intense field of energy pushing down on me, preventing me from getting up right away. Instead, I realised that I needed to sit quietly and withdraw gradually from this energy process.

As with the above two techniques, I also found that the technique of *La Qi* fitted in nicely with the others. After feeling the magnetic energy, I became aware of the fact that when I am breathing deeply and applying pressure on key energy points, I can feel the tingling magnetic energy sensation at different places. My acupressure session in turn prepares me to enter the ideal state of mind for pulling energy.

More than four months later, I can say that my objectivity routine has allowed me to better appreciate and practise some of the techniques that are utilised by Roger and Marcio. Even though I lack their expertise, wisdom and experience, I feel confident that in my work on Sebastien's body, I am able to transmit positive, healing energies. Most amazingly, I discovered that when I practise these techniques on him, I can experience the double benefits of calming myself and Sebastien down at the same time. Now that is what I call cost-effectiveness!

Considering the fact that I am not a professional specialist in any of the above techniques, I had wavered about whether I should write this chapter. Apart from deciding that I should share my own practice of these techniques and their benefits to encourage parents to follow likewise, I also realise that my modification of these techniques, especially with regard to their application to the autistic child, is entirely original.

Because Dr Hendricks and Mr Gach's target audience is the general public, their books did not take into consideration the resistance of many autistic children to unfamiliar touches. Many of these children are unlikely to sit still for you to apply firm pressure with your fingers on many of the important pressure points for 30 seconds or a minute. It is also difficult to teach our children how to do conscious breathing because many processes need to be coordinated at the same time.

Having experienced their benefits, however, I was determined to share them with Sebastien, somehow. So I came up with my own system of doing acupressure for him and teaching him how to do conscious breathing.

TECHNIQUES: The Modification Package

Familiarise yourself with the techniques first.
In order to know how all the above breathing and acupressure techniques work, you should try them on yourself several times first, until you have achieved a certain degree of familiarity with them.

There are two reasons for following this obvious suggestion. First of all, you need to know how they feel in order to determine which ones are likely to be tolerated and then accepted by your child. Only when you have personally experienced their beneficial effects will you be motivated in the long term to pursue this goal.

Second and more importantly, you need to be able to perform the techniques accurately on yourself before you can execute them on your child. You cannot be flipping through the book and reading the detailed instructions, while your child flees from you in the meantime. Make sure that when you do work on your child, you already have a firm grasp of the acupressure points and the targeted areas on your child. You can just go directly to these areas of your interest when using Mr Gach's book.

Prepare the body: the modification of acupressure.

As I had pointed out, most autistic children are unlikely to be cooperative in letting you apply firm pressure on specific points in any parts of their body, particularly the face, head, neck, shoulders and upper back. Unfortunately, many important pressure points that deal with the three common ailments experienced by autistic children are located there.

Instead of throwing out the entire package of acupressure, I decided to modify the acupressure techniques for Sebastien. Rather than use individual fingers to apply pressure on specific points, I only massaged or rubbed the relevant areas gently with my hands and palms without striving to pinpoint the specific points.

Parents in my training programme have raised this highly relevant question: "Will the acupressure techniques still be effective?" The answers are both "Yes" and "No."

According to Mr Gach, the acupressure techniques will only be effective when they are applied in accordance with his instructions of applying firm pressure on the specific points with the fingers, not massaging them. Therefore, I will concede the point that the massage method will not yield as effective a result as the correct way of administering acupressure.

Nonetheless, this does not mean that the massaging method in the key areas will yield zero benefits. In fact, if you study the acupressure book rather closely, you will notice that several acupressure points are clustered in close proximity to one another. Thus, with the broad movements, you can actually push on different acupressure points at the same time. Based on my observations of practitioners such as sensory integration therapists, Roger and Marcio, I can see that broad movements on specific areas can yield beneficial results of modulating the nervous system and the emotions of autistic children. So I can say that the massage method is still beneficial in its own right.

Even more importantly, I consider the massage method not to be the 'be-all and the end-all' of acupressure for autistic children. Rather, I consider it to be the precursor to acupressure. The massaging method is simply used to decrease our children's sensitivity to the touches in the specific areas and prepare their body for more concentrated work in the future. Essentially, what I tried to do was to chip away at Sebastien's resistance bit by bit by repeatedly exposing him to touches in the different areas such as his head. Over the period of three months, he became so habituated to feeling my hands on the back of his head, his forehead, his neck and his shoulders that he was no longer fidgeting and fighting my intrusion into his space. Four months later, I was able to use my fingers to hold the acupressure points with my fingers for a quick count of 10 and then 20.

Focus on what your child can do: the teaching of conscious breathing.
Breathing through the nose, as you know, is a very subtle process to explain to an autistic child with limited language skills. Back when I was searching for physiological strategies to help Sebastien to calm down before succumbing to his aggressive impulses, I tried to teach him how to breathe. Although he tried to follow what I was doing, he was only heaving his chest up and down, without breathing through his nose. So needless to say, I gave up.

After reading the conscious breathing book, however, I tried a new method of teaching Sebastien to breathe, which was fun and nurturing. Laying his body against mine, such that his belly was pressed against mine, I executed the exaggerated movements of deep breathing through my diaphragm. At the same time, I had him place his hands on my back so that he could feel the effects of the rise and fall of my back. Allowing him to experience the process of deep breathing in such a tactile and kinesthetic fashion was instrumental in helping him to grasp the practice of conscious breathing. While he still does not get the connection between the inhalation through the nose and the movements of the chest and the diaphragm, he has learnt how to move the rest of his body in the breathing process. To me, this is a significant improvement and a precursor to his ability to engage in conscious breathing in the future.

Seize the opportunities to use these strategies.
Many parents of autistic children pride themselves on having multiple types of learning and therapeutic programmes for their children. Apart from a learning programme and traditional therapeutic interventions such as speech therapy and occupational therapy, these children may also have a yoga programme and a Brain gym programme. The last thing I want you to do is to add the acupressure programme to your child's already bursting list of tasks and therapeutic activities.

What I would suggest is that you incorporate these acupressure procedures into your lives, without making it another structured activity. In other words, while you may consider it to be another beneficial activity for your child, he or she does not need to know about it. For example, when your child is doing academic work and seems distracted, you can then massage his or her memory and concentration points on the head and forehead. When you see your child getting anxious, you massage his or her neck and shoulders. Over time, you should become so familiar with the acupressure points that you will be able to fully benefit from the portability of these strategies and techniques by utilising them anytime and anywhere to deal with any situations.

The incorporation of these gentle massages and the acupressure strategies into our lives has allowed me to bond with Sebastien and spend quality time with him in all types of settings. Listening to the free live performances on the Waterfront near the Esplanade in Singapore, I would wrap my arms around his body in a protective embrace and move my hands gently on his head and shoulders in order to help him to modulate his exposure to the loud music and the environmental sounds. At the same time, he leans to me and presses his cheek against mine to benefit from the deep pressure of this contact. Whether Sebastien senses our connection or not, I will never know for certain. But my gut instinct tells me to treasure these beautiful moments. And I do.

Chapter Eight
Thriving in Mainstream Society: The Art of Interacting with Educational Institutions, Government Agencies and the General Public

PHILOSOPHY: The Top 10 Tenets

You are an expert...on your child.

Let me repeat. You are an expert...on your child, no matter what anyone else says. And if you are not, you need to be.

The truth is that all parents, whether they are those who can afford to pay for a wide range of services or those who cannot, play key roles in raising their children. I call us the 'headquarters' that is responsible for the coordination of all the different 'departments' (the educators and therapists) in our children's lives. We alone are aware of all the diverse treatments, programmes and activities, which are a part of our children's lives. Essentially, if we are not directly involved in the provision of the services, we need to know what is going on so that we can communicate to another therapist about the other current therapeutic activities in our children's lives.

For the many of us who can only afford services once or twice a week, please understand that these weekly or twice-a-week visits to the professionals are inadequate. In the US, even with the government funding and assistance provided, all professionals will tell parents that they still bear the primary responsibility of working with their children on a daily basis. Good professionals in my lives such as the occupational therapists I met in Los Angeles always spent the last 10 minutes of the sessions talking with me. They not only spoke about the outcomes of the sessions, but also demonstrated some of the techniques that I should implement at home. These professionals all know that no government will be able to subsidise the level of treatment needed by our children and not many parents in countries who did not get subsidies can often afford to pay for the necessary treatments.

Financial reasons aside, the reality is that parents or other primary caregivers are the only ones who see and interact with their children in a wide variety of settings. Considering the fact that autistic children often compartmentalise their world so that they modulate their behaviours in accordance with the individuals and their settings, it is evident that only parents are best able to construct a 'full' and 'complex' portrait of their children. This portrait is often far more complex and richer than the images generated by professionals who only see our children in therapeutic settings with perspectives that are heavily influenced by their specialised disciplines.

Finally, even though some autistic children may not show it, they do crave the love and attention of their parents. I strongly believe that all the care and attention devoted to a child by a professional or a school teacher will not outweigh the failure of parents to properly love and raise their autistic children. The extraordinary parent-child bonding is critical in the development of autistic children.

Let's say that you are already an expert on your child, like the way I have described it in the previous paragraphs. This is not the end of the story. Know that you will have to fight to assert your 'expert' status. In the US, the parent is nominally considered an equal member on the Individualised Education Plan Team; our input is supposed to have as much value as those of the other professionals on the team—the Special Education teacher, the General Education teacher, the School Psychologist, the Occupational Therapist, the Speech Therapist, the School Vice-Principal (typically the head of the Special Education Department) and the School District Official.

In reality, however, some of these professionals with their own specific agenda (whatever they may be), will not hesitate to try to impose their wishes on us parents. We are made to feel that they are the experts and we are just parents. Because the fields of autism and other developmental disorders have become specialised, with the involvement of many highly-trained professionals, parents who lack the specialised training have a distinctive disadvantage in all of these negotiations.

To advocate for your child, you must not be cowed by the professionals' knowledge and their privileged position. You must be willing to speak up and fight for what is best for your child. Even though all these professionals will say that they are looking out for the best interests of your child, trust me, their interests are often compromised by other competing factors and issues, which have little to do with your child.

The only adult who has the best interests of your child at heart in these discussions is YOU. Your child is counting on you to fight for his or her best interests.

Meet your child halfway.

I cannot tell you how frustrated I feel in my dialogues with some parents of autistic children in Singapore when they just lament about the fact that their children often embarrass them in school settings by acting inappropriately. Here is one such exchange:

Parent: *My son just kicked the teacher. It is so horrible.*

Kah Ying: *What happened?*

Parent: *I don't know.*

Kah Ying: *Did you ask the teacher?*

Parent: *They said they don't know. He just kicked the teacher.*

Kah Ying: *What happened before he kicked the teacher?*

Parent: *The teacher told him that the break was over. He ignored her. So she just took his lunch box away. Then he just kicked the teacher.*

Kah Ying: *And the teacher does not know why your son kicked her?*

Parent: *I know he has been unhappy with the teacher at the school. It was much better last year. The teacher this year is always complaining about him and saying why he cannot be just like the others.*

Kah Ying: *The teacher does not sound as though she has the right attitude by comparing the kids. She also did not act respectfully to your son when she just took his lunch box like that.*

(The parent is nodding away, as though in agreement...")
Parent: *But I don't know why he is kicking the teacher. He should not do that.*

This parent 'resolved' the crisis by simply telling her son not to kick the teacher again. The teacher, of course, did not have to make any changes to her behaviour.

While I am not condoning the child's act of aggression towards the teacher, I believe that it is vital for the parent to dig beneath the surface and go beyond the one-sided account of the teacher. Since the child was not able to present his account in as coherent a fashion as the teacher, the parent should be have played the part of an investigator and asked questions that would enable to determine what actually happened, even though she had not personally witnessed the incident. The 'Antecedent-Event-Consequence' Paradigm described in Chapter Five can certainly be applied to the school setting.

Guiding Questions:
- What is the event?
- What happened to trigger the event? (antecedent)
- What did the teacher do in response to the event? (consequence)
- How effective was the teacher's response to the event?
- If not, what other responses would have been more appropriate?

When teachers and parents dwell on the event in and of itself, they lay the complete blame on the offending child. The only solution: the child should just behave himself. By failing to address the underlying causes of the child's offending behaviour, however, it is highly unlikely that the child will change his or her behaviour. The truth is, in this instance, there were several reasons that could have caused the child to kick the teacher:

- The child does not like the teacher who treats him poorly.

- The teacher acted in an inappropriate way by taking away the child's lunch box container without informing the child of her impending action.

- There may be other factors within the general classroom setting such as the behaviours of the other children, the quality of the school work and the sensory challenges of the environment, which may also be increasing the child's tendency to engage in aggression.

In this instance, not only should the child be expected to change his behaviour, but the teacher should also be asked to improve her interaction style. Both parties should have been asked to reach a compromise and meet one another halfway.

As parents, we tend to get so mortified by our children's behaviour that we do not want to be accused of being a biased parent by defending them in any way. In leaping to the other side so quickly, however, we are unfair to our children when we expect them to accommodate people in the mainstream society, whether the latter has acted appropriately or inappropriately. By doing so, we are actually governed by an inherent bias against our children. Whether we are conscious of this fact or not, we are inherently biased against our children because we are 'typical'.

In straddling the two boats, we must really learn how to take into consideration the competing sides of both parties. While parents in the US often err by setting unreasonable expectations for teachers and schools, their counterparts in Singapore fail to properly represent their children's interests by conceding to the teachers and the schools all too readily. In my opinion, neither the child nor the teacher or school should be expected to cave in completely. Rather, a merry compromise that takes into account the interests of both sides should be achieved.

You will always pay the price.
Just in case advocating for your child sounds a little too hard, inconvenient, or complex, let me give you an additional incentive: You will always pay the price. Whether a school teacher or a therapist has treated your child poorly, your child will always hold you ultimately responsible for these transgressions.

The most obvious reason is that you have put your child in the setting and have thus allowed the transgression to occur. You are essentially the 'mastermind' behind this situation. When parents fail to intervene on behalf of their children in these crises, their children feel betrayed and let down (by their parents). For autistic children with limited social contact, their first lesson of disillusionment with their parents can shape their entire perspective of typical people. Thus, in a sense, we also play an important role in being representatives of mainstream society in the eyes of our autistic children.

Another obvious reason is that at the end of the day, our children will come home to us and bring with them their accumulated baggage of negative emotions as a result of their unsatisfactory relationships with the outside world. Because they cannot articulate their feelings properly to their parents, many of them are unable to vent their fury, frustration and sadness. Over time, these pent-up feelings that are trapped in their beings may erupt in a dramatic, uncontrolled and unpredictable fashion. Sebastien's initial aggression in response to the oppressive behaviours of his first one-on-one aide in kindergarten is a consequence of my failure to act swiftly and effectively on behalf of him. However inconvenient it was for me, I should have removed him from the classroom. But I did not and I paid the price.

Most importantly, I believe that our advocacy for our children— our willingness to fight for their rights—lies at the heart of our relationship with our children. Although they may not seem to notice or show their appreciation in obvious ways, our children, with their heightened intuitive sense, know when we are fighting for them. By proving our love and concern for them through our actions, we encourage our children to place their trust in us. For our children, we are literally their window to the mainstream world. Whether and how they will take their tentative steps into the mainstream world will be inextricably interwoven with how we relate to people and the institutions in mainstream society.

APPROACH

As advocates for our children, we parents are often regarded as biased individuals who are taking the side of our children. There is nothing wrong with this fact. In any negotiations, each of the parties involved has a specific agenda. In approaching any type of negotiations, however, we can increase the likelihood of our success by presenting our viewpoints and our perspectives in a non-adversarial manner and putting forth win-win ideas and solutions. In other words, the compromise solution I am advocating above needs to be couched in terms that allows parties to feel that they have 'won' in some way or another in this negotiation.

To offer a concrete example of this approach, let me revert to the previous example of the child who has just kicked the teacher. In striving to get the teacher to adjust her behaviour and attitude, I would highlight how much easier her task of dealing with the child would be if she would simply follow some of these instructions. Understand that in order to be able to do this, you have to be an expert on your child and know strategies that do work for your child to elicit good behaviour. Back when Sebastien was in his younger years, my 'no meany face' approach to dealing with his aggression scored points with professionals who marvelled at its effectiveness in curtailing his aggression. In other words, you have to have good ideas about your child, which do work, to encourage the teacher to pursue your strategy.

At the same time, the mother should let the teacher know how she intends to help her son modify his behaviour. The teacher, therefore, should not harbour any belief that she alone is expected to change. By sharing her strategy with the teacher, the mother lets the teacher know that she appreciates the teacher's willingness to collaborate with her in implementing the game plan to ensure its consistency and effectiveness. Please note that the mother should not be saying and doing all these things to pacify the teacher. She needs to be actually implementing the game plan because she has to deal with her son's inappropriate behaviours.

Evidently, there will be times when your approach, in spite of your best intentions, will not get you anywhere, because of the individual teacher or the general culture of the school environment. In such instances, I would cut my losses and remove your child from such an environment immediately. Knowing that you cannot be responsible for the reactions of others, you must constantly decide whether the investment of your energies in these negotiations is worthwhile, based on the likelihood of the success of your efforts.

IMPLEMENTATION: The Dos and Don'ts of Negotiations

Dos

1. Investigate, interrogate and navigate.

Just because you are not there does not mean that you have to take the teacher's word for it. All human beings are biased and subjective—an account from one person can only represent a single and limited perspective.

During one of my most nightmarish encounters with a teacher who had Asperger's Syndrome, he would often present a skewed account of what happened in order to absolve himself of any responsibility. He belonged to the 'blame the child' category of professionals by dwelling on what the child did, without making any effort to trace the underlying causes, particularly his role in contributing to the negative event.

I was fortunate to have a good relationship with Sebastien's outstanding one-on-one aide who cared enough about him to defy the oppressive nature of traditional school hierarchy to give me another account. Her far more comprehensive account included attempts to identify the underlying triggers that often illuminate the teacher's culpability in contributing to the event, and sometimes even her own. As a consequence, I realised that I could not rely on any single accounts, but judge each one of them on their merits in order to get as close to the truth as possible.

Therefore, if you still feel that you do not have the whole picture, ask as many people as you need to, until no additional information has come up. In order to do this, you may have to approach different people at different levels of the school hierarchy in order to get the information. Clearly, the level of your effort should match the importance of the event to you.

2. Go straight to the top... and make sure the people at the bottom know about it.

When your negotiations with the teacher at the classroom level fails, let the teacher know that you will approach the school principal —the next level on the school hierarchy. Since the teacher is the only one who is directly involved in the day-to-day dealings with your child, you will need to document the situation in writing when you approach the principal. Apart from describing the situation, you will also need to talk about all your efforts to resolve the situation to illustrate the teacher's unwillingness to cooperate with you.

At the bottom of this letter, please include a 'cc:' that will include a list of all the people to whom you have sent this letter. This list should include the teacher and more importantly, all the people who occupy higher positions than the school principal at the school district and ministry levels. Politicians who are responsible for the districts, as well as those who have shown a strong interest in education, should also be included.

This tiny little 'cc:' can do more than anything in motivating school principals to act swiftly to deal with the situation. Whether it be out of the fears of their superiors knowing about the situation or not, or the actual crackdown by their superiors, school principals will act and do their part in dealing with the teachers in order to resolve the situation. These are one of the few moments when parents can benefit from the rigidity of the chain of command that governs schools and government agencies.

What I had discovered when I learned about this strategy in the US was how much more willing those who occupied positions at the top were willing to accommodate me and deal with me in a respectful fashion than those in lower positions who were downright rude to me.

For example, when I wrote a letter to protest against the Santa Monica School District's attempt to force Sebastien to go to a shoddy school-based occupational therapy facility, in lieu of a good physical and occupational therapy clinic that he had been attending for the last three years, I got a letter of apology from the head of the school district office. A woman at the lower levels of the office, however, called to tell me off for telling on her to her boss. Although I was surprised by this reality, I immediately learned that professionals and administrators at higher levels of hierarchy are far more receptive to parents because they have so much more to lose when they lose their jobs.

3. Demand to know what is happening in the classroom and give your opinions.

Very often, parents are only informed of what is happening in the classroom only after their children have acted out. In my conversations with parents in Singapore, some of them told me that by the time the teacher talked to them about their children's poor behaviour, it had already gone on for several months. Given the fact that you cannot simply rely on the teacher's initiative to inform you of the situation, you must be proactive in keeping regular tabs on your child's progress.

In the US, parents and teachers have a communication book. This book is a vital tool that allows parents to learn about what is happening in the classroom on a daily basis. It also allows parents to let teachers know what is happening at home so that both parties can ensure that an integrated and consistent strategy is implemented across all settings.

While I was living in Los Angeles, however, I noticed that the teachers often did not write in the books so that I could not even be sure that they had read my entries, thus defeating its purpose. On the other hand, in Phoenix, Arizona, the teacher wrote in the book every single day. In some cases, the one-on-one aides stepped in to fill in the gap, which was also sufficient.

At the time, it is also important for parents to be realistic about how much the teacher can write in these books because they must insert entries for 10 kids at the end of the day. Therefore, if you need more detailed accounts, you should just contact them directly by phone or e-mail, depending on the urgency of the situation. If it is sufficiently important or serious, you should schedule a meeting with the teacher after school.

What I often emphasise to parents in my parent training programme is that it is vital for parents to cultivate a relationship with the teachers and show their active monitoring of their children's situation in schools. As I tell them, if the teacher knows that the child has a parent who is actively monitoring the child's progress in school and who is willing to fight for the child, this teacher will treat the child with considerably more respect. While it would be ideal if we can forge close, friendly relationships with our children's teachers (I had such a relationship with Sebastien's teacher in Phoenix), we may not be so lucky all the time. In these instances, if we choose to leave our children in the same classroom setting, we must be ever more vigilant in voicing our demands and asserting ourselves on behalf of our children.

4. Exercise your right as a parent.

As a parent of your autistic child, you need to exercise your right fully in order to fight for your child's rights. In Singapore, that is characterised by an acute and chronic lack of basic and support services for children with autism, parents have come to accept the sub-quality of services, poor bedside manner on the part of professionals ranging from specialists at hospitals to teachers in special needs schools and the current state of affairs. This level of disempowerment effectively means that parents have willingly relinquished their rights to obtain a decent level of education for their children with autism and decent customer service standards.

By hanging our heads down in defeat and resigning ourselves to the situation, we are transmitting the wrong messages to our children and to the mainstream society. We let our children down by letting them think that the quality of education or services provided to them is adequate when it is not. Just as significantly, we perpetuate the illusion that the education and the support of families with autistic children are sufficient when it cannot be further from the truth.

5. Reach out... You are not alone.

Many cultures have proverbs of some kind that basically extols this important message: there is strength in numbers. Living in a mainstream society (both in the US and Singapore), there are many parents who consider their child's autism to be a stigma, something to be ashamed of and hidden away. Parents in my parent training programme are often surprised to encounter their former colleagues during the sessions and learn that the latter's children also have autism.

This 'hush-hush' approach only serves to amplify the already intensely lonely experience of raising an autistic child. The truth is that just as with life, there is really no one else who can fully empathise with you about your child or your experience, even though they may have an autistic child. In my encounters with various parents and their autistic children, I can see that each child cannot be more different than another. Concomitantly, the challenges faced by parents also differ considerably from one another.

Nonetheless, parents of autistic children are better able to understand the plight of those like them than parents with typical children. Together, parents of autistic children have to face the battle of finding out and getting the right educational and therapeutic services for their children. As a group, they know how it feels like to work with unresponsive and ineffective professionals and educators. They have also experienced the embarrassment of their children's inappropriate behaviours and endured the stares and dirty looks of the members of the general public.

In terms of advocacy, parents who link up with others can get together to voice their concerns as a group in order to present a petition. This approach is particularly effective with politicians who are concerned with garnering the votes of the people. The strength in numbers has a literal advantage. While one parent crying out in protest may be dismissed as an insignificant whine from a kitten, a large group of parents doing the same thing will create quite a racket—one that cannot be as easily dismissed.

Moreover, parents as a whole can often exchange information about good ideas and strategies, as well as provide actual support for one another in advocacy situations. Inspired by the group dynamics, parents in group situations can often feed off the energy of one another and offer novel ideas that are extremely helpful to other parents.

Some of these strategies and approaches that I have described in this book are products of what I have learnt in my group advocacy efforts with these mothers who were formerly lawyers until they quit the practice to devote their lives to their children.

Don'ts

1. Do not be desperate.

When you are desperate, you naturally place yourself in a disadvantageous position in any negotiation. This is the situation in Singapore where the demand for any types of services far surpasses the supply. Parents, particularly those who can only afford to attend the government-subsidised schools, are often so grateful to finally get a place in the schools— after waiting for months on the waiting list—that they dare not question or negotiate with teachers. The constant refrain—'It is better than nothing' or 'At least, he is getting educated in school'— are excuses that parents use to assuage their own feelings of guilt and their gut reaction that their children are not getting the appropriate treatment.

2. Do not take 'I don't know' for an answer.

If you ever encounter this response from any professionals when you are asking them about your child, do not resign yourself to the situation. Speak up and ask questions. The fact is that educators working with your child should not get away with a 'I don't know' answer. If they were not there or did not witness it directly, they should go out of their way to help you locate the people who would know. If not, it is up to you to investigate and identify the people who can help you. And if you find that you are not getting any help or support, it is time to go straight to the top.

What I am really trying to emphasise is that there is a minimum standard of behaviour and expectations that should be met by professionals in their work with our children. We parents should not be expected to continue to lower our standards and expectations to the point where we feel helpless and resigned to our fates.

As I had mentioned before, you will pay the price, whether in the form of a feisty protesting child who is acting out constantly, or worse still, a depressed and indifferent child who has lost his faith in the world, in you and in his own future. Having met autistic children who fall into these categories, I can tell you that in all these instances, the parents have accepted their children's educators' 'I don't know' responses.

3. Do not be afraid to be unpopular.

One of the first lessons that I learned in the US as a mother of an autistic child is that those who are quiet and accept all that is offered by the agencies without asking for more will get just what they are offered. And believe me, public agencies that are always strapped by a lack of sufficient public funding will only give you the barest minimum. While you may think that they just do not have enough to give you, I will say that this is a matter of allocation of scarce funds. In the waiting rooms of therapy facilities, I have heard many parents who show off about their notoriety among professionals and agencies for their requests for funding of all types of interventions and services, which are not typically funded by government agencies. Yet, by pestering these public agencies on a regular basis and even hiring lawyers to fight their cases, these parents always manage to get more than their fair share of funding.

Although there is a part of me that is resentful at the selfishness of these parents for getting funding for these extra services while other families are deprived of the basic ones, I have also learned from them. While I am far more reasonable in my expectations than such parents, I do make requests for services and ask about service providers that have been recommended to me by other parents. This type of information will not be volunteered by the caseworker. Only when I asked her about the specific service provider did she confirm his or her availability. For example, even though she knew that I was looking for a good speech therapist, the caseworker did not volunteer the information about any speech therapists that was funded by the government.

Over the course of the years of fighting for Sebastien in distressing school situations, I had learnt that it is fine to be unpopular for a good cause and your child definitely counts as one. While I had assumed that all parents would fight just as hard for their children if they knew about their children's distressing situation, I was wrong. In Singapore, I encountered many parents who actually asked me whether it was alright for them to offer the teachers their suggestions and challenge them in various ways. I told them that this was a question that would never be asked by a parent in the US.

Therefore, I realise that the Asian culture that prioritises the collective harmony over the individual interest is particularly detrimental to parents of autistic children because they need to be individuals who dare to stand up above the crowd and scream for attention. We parents are not attention seekers; we scream for attention because the minimum level of standards and services has not been met.

While living in the US, there were school principals, vice-principals, teachers and students who knew me intimately because I was constantly forced to go to the school to fight for my son. At the same time, there were other schools in which none of the administrative personnel knew me in person because the teacher was doing an adequate job. Trust me, the adults in the former category of schools did not like me. Some of them imposed time limits on me according to the law and told me that I had to leave the classroom in 20 minutes. Still, I persisted and I fought hard for Sebastien, until I could make a change.

As a result of these difficult years of fighting for my son, I had become strengthened. From a weak and docile mother who was brought up not to inconvenience people, I became good at 'inconveniencing' people and speaking up to professionals and people in authority when needed. I did things that terrified me, such as public speaking, but I overcame that fear at a school district meeting that was televised citywide in order to fight for Sebastien's rights. There were many parents who chose not to speak up in these instances, for whatever reasons. In retrospect, I am glad that I stood up and won an important victory for my son. Even more importantly, four years after that event, when the decision was no longer important to Sebastien or to me, I could see how important it has been in my journey to empower myself as a mother of an autistic child.

4. Do not be ashamed of your child.

I think one of the reasons why parents find it hard to advocate for their children is because they are basically ashamed of them—ashamed of the latter's strange behaviours and weird mannerisms. Mortified by their children's behaviours that make them stick out like sore thumbs, these parents are often quick to empathise with the educators and professionals when they complain. All these parents are willing to do is to pacify these educators and professionals in order to ensure that their children can still remain in the school. By doing so, they think that they have done the best for their children.

To me, this lowering of expectations and standards of the people who work with our children is so damaging to the psyche of ourselves and our children. How can we expect outsiders to treat our children with a decent measure of respect and integrity if we ourselves do not embrace them for who they are? In doing so, we give poor professionals the license to continue to act inappropriately and undermine any prospects of improvement for our children.

Therefore, an integral part of advocacy stems from the need for parents to turn inward and examine themselves in an honest fashion. We must identify the beliefs and perceptions that shape our opinions of our children. In this heartwrenching process, we may discover that, though we profess our love for them, we entertain many thoughts and feelings, which cannot be considered to be loving or unconditional in any way.

So if you discover that you are ashamed of your child, please talk to someone about it and deal with your feelings of shame. Do not let your shame destroy your love for your child and his or her life.

CONCLUDING THOUGHTS

We have arrived at the end of this phase of my thus-far incredible journey with Sebastien. I hope that you have acquired some insights and information, which would prove to be worthwhile in your own journey with your autistic child. Honestly, nothing can prepare you for the trials and heartbreaks that will arise during this journey. Yet, as you grieve the loss of your fantasised notion of a typical child, along with your dreams for his or her future, do not ever forget that your plight is a zillion times better than that of your child.

Regardless of the difficulties you encounter and experience as a parent, you have to understand that what your child is going through is far more difficult. After all, our autistic children are the ones who have to struggle with their deficits and overcome them in the best possible way they know how. They alone bear the *onus* of having to live in a world that will mock them for their inability to express themselves appropriately, or behave in ways that conform to society's norms. Even though we as parents can do our very best to lighten their burdens, there is no doubt that our children face an uphill battle each and every day. Reminding ourselves each day about this essential reality will really help us to keep our grief in perspective.

In looking over the past eight years, I realise that I would not wish them away for all the money in the world. I feel that I have been blessed beyond measure by having Sebastien in my life, autism and all. As a parent who has suffered and struggled with Sebastien's deficits, I know far too well how easy it would be to dwell on them and wallow in fears of his future.

For me, however, I can only be amazed by the incredible progress Sebastien has made up the steep hill of his life. Year after year, he has continued to impress me with his unique perspectives and gifts. In the last few months, with my own awakening to my own inadequacies as an individual and a mother, I have been even more conscious of the value of Sebastien's unique strengths.

With the help of inspiring friends with unique perspectives about people with special needs, including Roger and Marcio, I can finally acknowledge Sebastien's utilisation of his acute visual and auditory sensitivity to help him distinguish one MRT station from another. Through his sudden interest in the pottery wheel, I have discovered that he possesses tremendous strength and control in his hands as he forms and shapes the wet clay in his hands on the pottery wheel, while my efforts spiral away and disintegrate.

Yet, even more important than all these accomplishments is his perseverance as he trudges up the hill each and every day. His never-say-die attitude in his willingness to make tentative forays into the unknown and his unflinching passion for the hustle and bustle of daily life have inspired me tremendously. They testify to the strength of his spirit and courage.

Through my journey with Sebastien, I know that I have received far more from him than I have given. My life has been transformed and enriched by the presence of an extraordinary child. Yes, Sebastien is an extraordinary child. I take that over 'typical' or 'normal' any day.

Now it is your turn to open your eyes and love your extraordinary child before you.

APPENDICES

Appendix 1
Profile of Your Child

GENERAL INSTRUCTIONS

When completing this profile, please support each of your responses with concrete and detailed examples of your child's behaviour and activity. Like a private investigator, you must be able to 'prove' what you are saying. To give you an idea of what I am talking about, check out my profile of Sebastien (Appendix 2).

Clearly, the space allotted in this book will not be enough for your profile. So, feel free to type it into your computer and insert the information there.

Do <u>not</u> rush to complete the profile.

The process of creating this profile is to help you reflect on your understanding of your child so that you will have a comprehensive profile of your child. Only with a comprehensive profile will you be successful in developing an appropriate learning programme for your child.

OVERALL ASSESSMENT

Identify the strengths and weaknesses of your child in terms of his or her personality, skills and potential for the future.

Strengths:

Weaknesses:

CURRENT LEVEL OF FUNCTIONING

Knowing the current level of functioning will help you to establish appropriate expectations of what your child can or cannot do at this moment in time. You will also be able to identify the most effective methods that will allow you to interact with your child successfully in a learning programme.

The current level of functioning of your child is evaluated in terms of: a) communication skills; b) living skills; c) sensory issues; and d) behavioural issues. Several guiding questions are listed under each section to jump-start this process for you. This list of questions is, by no means, exhaustive. Please feel free to move beyond them to pinpoint areas that are relevant to your child.

A. Communication Skills

Guiding questions:

1. Does your child speak only in single-word utterances and/or sentences?
2. Does he use language for non-communicative purposes?
3. Does he only make requests for items or can he also express his comments and observations?
4. Does he respond to your queries appropriately?
5. Does he stay on topic when he is conversing with others?
6. Does he make good eye contact and use appropriate body language to accompany what he says?
7. Can he interpret non-verbal communication?

B. Daily Living Skills

Guiding questions:

1. Does your child have age-appropriate self-care skills (eg. washing hands, brushing teeth, putting on clothes, etc.) for his or her age?
2. Does your child have age-appropriate practical skills for functioning in the public space (eg. riding the MRT and recognising the value of money)?
3. What are the different living skills that are difficult for your child? Why do you think that they are challenging for your child?

C. Sensory Issues
Guiding questions:
1. Is your child highly sensitive to human touch or textures of certain substances such as playdough, paint or whipped cream?
2. Is your child overly sensitive to sounds and sights? For example, does he cover his ears or watch things very closely?
3. Does your child lack a sense of how much pressure to exert when performing a task? For example, does he or she press too hard or too softly when writing?
4. Does your child struggle with implementing fine motor tasks? For example, does he experience difficulties with cutting?
5. Does your child require constant movement?
6. Does your child seem to require constant sensory stimulation such as crashing into body or objects?

These questions certainly do not cover all the sensory difficulties experienced by all autistic children. However, they serve as a starting point for helping you to observe your child in action and identify additional sensory difficulties.

D. Behavioural Issues
Guiding questions:
1. Does your child engage in tantrums or other disruptive behaviours in order to get what he wants?
2. Does your child pinch, hit, push, kick (and other aggressive behaviours) in order to get his way or just to vent his frustration?
3. Is your child non-compliant? Essentially, when you ask him to do something, he refuses to do it, even though he understands what you would like him to do.
4. Does your child engage in other socially inappropriate behaviours in the public space such as laughing excessively in a cinema?

A. Communication Skills:

_____

_____

_____

_____

_____

_____

_____

_____

_____

_____

_____

_____

_____

_____

_____

_____

_____

_____

B. Living Skills:

_____

_____

_____

_____

_____

_____

_____

_____

_____
_____
_____
_____
_____
_____
_____
_____
_____

C. Sensory Issues:

_____
_____
_____
_____
_____
_____
_____
_____
_____
_____
_____
_____
_____
_____
_____
_____
_____
_____

D. Behavioural Issues:

_____
_____
_____
_____
_____
_____
_____
_____
_____
_____
_____
_____
_____
_____
_____
_____
_____
_____
_____

INTERESTS, OBSESSIONS AND FIXATIONS

The most effective way to get your child interested in a learning programme is to incorporate his or her interests, obsessions and fixations into the diverse learning tasks. This strategy means that your child will be intrinsically motivated to participate in the tasks.

Many parents are often terrified of their children's obsessions and fixations. They will do anything to steer their children away from them. By exercising their dormant creativity, however, parents can actually gain some control over their children's interests, obsessions and fixations by offering them an appropriate outlet to channel them—learning activities.

These interests, obsessions and fixations will also constitute an invaluable source of inspiration for you to design an engaging curriculum for your child. Each of these interests can be recycled in different ways to help your child develop different skills.

Interests, Obsessions and Fixations:

_____

_____

_____

_____

_____

_____

_____

_____

_____

_____

_____

_____

_____

_____

_____

_____

_____

_____

_____

LEARNING STYLES AND PREFERENCES

In recent years, educators have come to realise that all children learn differently. Concomitantly, not all children are going to be responsive to the traditional type of teaching in which a teacher stands in front of the classroom and lectures the students.

For autistic children, the aural method of teaching is particularly difficult as they are highly visual learners who attend better to the learning task when it is presented visually either in images or written words. Many of them have difficulties with processing language, which makes it hard for them to hold onto the fleeting existence of spoken language. Learning materials presented in a visual format allow autistic children to look back and refer to the information as many times as they need.

Autistic children also prefer contextualised learning approaches, in contrast to decontextualised learning. Contexts offer background information and descriptions that allow autistic children to visualise scenarios and situations presented in the learning task, thus making it far more concrete and meaningful for them. For example, in Sebastien's case, I offer him contextual information by relating his learning tasks to his routines, environments and interests.

Interests, Obsessions and Fixations:

Appendix 2
Sebastien's Profile

DESCRIPTION

Strengths:
Sebastien possesses a strong visual memory about locations. Specifically, he seems to have a three-dimensional visual perspective of places, which are present in other autistic adults such as Temple Grandin who have written about their visual skills. In Sebastien's case, I notice that he studies the relative locations of buildings and other features in the general environment closely so as to recognise their unique characteristics. With this ability, he is able to figure out the home station during his second trip on the Mass Rapid Transit (MRT) within his first week in Singapore. Furthermore, he could often recall the locations of new places of interest at vacation spots three months later without relying on signs or conventional clues.

Sebastien exhibits a strong curiosity about his surrounding environment. In recent months, his curiosity in his environment is apparent in his focused observation of human and systemic activity. He is particularly interested in activities that follow repetitive sequences and steps. Moreover, he has also been able to participate in performing three-step household and administrative tasks at home. To me, his focused attention to detail and deviations from the system makes him an outstanding, if not a tyrannous, Quality Control (QC) supervisor!

As with other autistic people I have encountered, Sebastien is very directed and focused. He knows what he wants and will not deviate from his path until he has achieved his goals. In spite of his limited language skills, he often astounds me by his efforts to communicate his needs and wants to others in order to achieve his goals.

Sebastien is a survivor. Several years ago, I was reduced to uncontrollable tears, while watching a movie entitled *Mercury Rising*. In this movie, a non-verbal autistic child's parents were murdered. At the time, it was terrifying for me to imagine how Sebastien would survive in this world without me. Over the last few years, I had discovered that Sebastien, with his strong survival instincts, would know how to act nicely to the available caregiver to ensure that his needs are met. For example, when I left him with his babysitter for a weekend to attend a church retreat, she remarked that he treated her nicer than ever before, because he was not sure whether I would be coming back!

Sebastien possesses a strong intuition about people. Since he was a toddler, he has always been able to evaluate people. While he cooperated nicely with fun and caring therapists, he would throw a huge tantrum with professionals he did not like from the very first day. Back then, I had only considered his behaviour to be a huge inconvenience when he rejected the therapist on the very first day.

Also, I had wrongly assumed that he was only attracted to young and pretty female therapists. It just so happened that many of the occupational therapists whom he liked fell under this category. In recent years, however, I have seen him embrace old and/or unattractive (in appearance) men and women and I realise that his perceptions penetrate far beneath the surface.

He is highly motivated and industrious. Contrary to what most people think about autistic people who often avoid doing work or learning tasks, autistic people can be extremely motivated. The misconception about autistic children as unwilling learners stems from the fact that they often do not understand what is expected of them when they are given conventional learning tasks.

A few years ago, I was surprised to find that Sebastien would actually clamour for more homework once he understood what was expected of him. These days, I in turn surprise people by telling them that Sebastien would rather do 'homework' with me than do nothing at all.

Sebastien is extremely passionate about life. One of the things that truly inspires me about him is his passion for living. In spite of all his deficits that make life extremely challenging for him, Sebastien is always raring to get his day started and dismayed at the end of the day when it is time to sleep. For many typical people who are bored by the monotony of his routines, Sebastien considers his routines and his familiar surrounding to be comforting.

Because of his attention to detail, he is able to perceive changes and differences in his surroundings, which may not be remarkable, noticeable or conspicuous in the eyes of typical people. As an example, Sebastien does not consider the uniform MRT route from one location to another to be dull and monotonous. From his point of view, each ride is distinguished from another by the composition of the commuters in the MRT and on the platform; the changes in the weather conditions; the unpredictability of the movements of the MRT with its occasional jolting motion; and the oncoming train coming on a different track from the opposite direction. Any one or more of these factors is sufficient to make the MRT ride on the same route a new and exciting one.

Weaknesses:
Sebastien has limited language skills that are many years behind his peers. Although he has made tremendous progress in the recent months and years, he continues to exhibit difficulties with processing language, particularly at the spoken level. His spontaneous spoken language, at this point, is still limited to one- to two-word utterances. The fact that he can read and write far better than he can speak testifies to his difficulties in processing language when he does not have the opportunity to revisit the language visually.

Sebastien has a high level of frustration. Because of the incompatibility between the thoughts in his mind and his ability to express them, he experiences a high level of frustration. He is easily frustrated in situations that are confusing or uncertain to him because he knows that he cannot ask for clarification, thus illuminating his language difficulties. He also gets angry when he is corrected, or asked to make corrections—another situation that highlights his inadequacies.

He has strong aggression tendencies. He feels justified in venting his frustration with aggression. Although he has come a long way in coping with his aggression, he still requires constant reminders when he is mad and frustrated to deter him from reverting instinctively to aggression.

He is still fundamentally clueless about social cues. Even though he has become more aware of me as someone who interacts closely with him on a daily basis, he is still oblivious to many of his social transgressions. He still does not understand why appearing naked in public is a shocking thing, or why it is not acceptable to push people in front of him out of the way.

Sebastien's facial affect and eye contact are still noticeably flat and inconsistent, compared to typical individuals. Even though he displays considerably more animation and life in his facial expressions and eyes than before, he is still difficult to read and interpret. It takes a discerning person who is familiar with his expressions to know when he is growing distressed and frustrated.

CURRENT LEVEL OF FUNCTIONING

Communication Skills:
Currently, Sebastien's spontaneous utterances are still limited to one to two words, even as their number has increased gradually over the years. With verbal prompting, he can speak in full sentences. His understanding of questions is still rather limited, though he is definitely making an effort to understand what is being said.

My conversations with him are still limited to routines and requests for items or actions. Through social scripts, he has learned to say "Thank you," "You are welcome," and greet others appropriately, though he continues to require some guidance.

Nonetheless, Sebastien has a strong awareness of the communicative function of language. Therefore, unlike many of his autistic counterparts with far stronger language skills, he does not utilise language in inappropriate ways such as 'verbal stimming.' 'Verbal stimming'—a form of self-talk—not only fails to serve a communicative function, but it also enables autistic people to shut out others, while they are engaged in their world of self-talk. When Sebastien uses language, it is strictly for communication purposes.

Furthermore, Sebastien has somehow understood the to-and-fro patterns of conversation. Even when he does not understand what I have said, he would reply, "Yes," as though he is imitating what he has observed in typical human conversations.

Finally, he has a strong command of non-verbal communication. He often uses his eyes and gestures to indicate what he wants. More common than not, he is effective in achieving his objectives, even with people who are unfamiliar with him, such as new adult acquaintances.

Living Skills:
At this juncture, he can independently perform most self-care skills with verbal guidance, feedback and minimum support. These self-care skills include getting dressed, washing hands, brushing teeth and taking a shower. Furthermore, he is a great helper in performing certain household tasks such as folding the laundry and hanging wet clothes.

Currently, I am capitalising on his interest in his environment to introduce him to the MRT system and the traffic lights. For example, at the MRT station, I show him the MRT map and the TV that indicates when the MRT is arriving. I point out signs and ask him to show me where I need to go.

Sensory Challenges:
Sebastien continues to exhibit sensitivities to the environment because he is unable to tune out his environment both visually

and aurally. Unlike typical people who have the automatic ability to ignore aspects of their environment, he can see and hear many things in the environment. As a result, he is easily overwhelmed by all the outside stimuli.

Lacking in his ability to express and vent his emotions in a socially appropriate way, he still struggles with regulating his emotions. For instance, he can display radical swings of emotions from one extreme to another (crying in one instant followed by laughing in the next instant). During these episodes, he may require 30 minutes or more to settle down and regain his composure.

Behavioural Issues:
In spite of the fact that Sebastien no longer manifests any form of aggression, especially towards orders, I strongly believe that the aggression tendency is still very much present in him. Therefore, he still needs to be managed carefully with frequent reminders for him to regulate his reactions to events and situations that are distressing or frustrating to him.

Due to his need to adhere to specific routines or his fear of transitions and new places, Sebastien may also be non-compliant and resistant. Because his language is still limited, he may try to get his way either through aggression or tantrumming. Therefore, he continues to require a system of consistent behavioural strategies and sensory techniques.

Interests, Obsessions and Fixations:
Based on my observations, Sebastien is a passionate lover of machines and systems. Because machines and systems often follow a repetitive sequence, they are predictable and controllable in his eyes. This feeling of control and predictability exerts a calming influence on him—a means for him to defuse his stress from the unpredictability of human life, which is far more challenging for him.

He is also a hands-on person who enjoys various kinds of sensory input: the feeling of wet sand between his fingers and his toes; the relaxing pressure on his neck and head, while doing shoulder stands; the calm movement of water in the swimming pool; the sensation of little morsels of rice and noodles in his fingers, etc.

Learning Styles and Preferences:
Overall, I will describe Sebastien as a visual, tactile and kinesthetic learner. In other words, he learns best when he is able to match his learning tasks to visual images. At the same time, if he is able to touch and manipulate the learning materials, the learning experience will be even more interesting to him. He also learns very well when movements are incorporated into the learning activity. Therefore, visual and hands-on activities play a strong role in his learning programme.

He shows a definite preference for contextualised learning. The juxtaposition of his learning tasks with routines and favourite activities captures his attention and lends meaning to his learning programme. Even though he may have a little difficulty with the learning task, he is able to make references to his real-life experiences to bolster his understanding and interest in the activity.

Appendix 3
Highlights of Sebastien's Learning Programme

- Regardless of the learning objectives I have, the presentation of each of the learning tasks is explicitly designed to match Sebastien's learning styles and preferences, as well as his interests.

- When Sebastien is given a language or mathematical task, which involves the learning of symbols and abstract concepts, he is aided with pictures of objects or actual objects to allow him to convert the abstract—something that is difficult for him—into something concrete and familiar.

- To further motivate Sebastien in his learning, I often design learning tasks around his favourite activities, places and interests. Typically, the learning tasks are derived from his real-life experiences. These favourite activities offer the inspiration for me to shape and design the learning activities in the form that would appeal to him, while incorporating my learning objectives for him.

- To lend variety to the tasks, I utilise a wide variety of materials for visual aids: brochures and maps from tourist atttactions; photographs and pictures from the Internet; drawings I made that can be cut out; stencils; 'peel & stick' window paint; photographs from my camera phone that can be uploaded onto the computer and downloaded; and video footages from the Internet.

- Instead of separating his learning tasks into separate disciplines (such as math, science or language), I design learning tasks that will allow Sebastien to acquire and hone a wide variety of skills: reading; writing; cutting; counting; attending to task; and typing on computer and using the mouse.

- I tailor each of the tasks to be slightly above the level of Sebastien's level of functioning. In other words, he will always require guidance from an adult to perform the tasks in order to help him to move forward. At the same time, they are not so difficult as to make him feel frustrated and discouraged.

- Finally, I want to emphasise the fact that the designing and the implementation of homework is a trial-and-error process, particularly when I am trying to teach a new skill or a new concept. Because I am designing a new presentation format and introducing a new skill to him, I am open to the likelihood that I will have to revise the learning task several times in response to his reactions to the tasks:

Is he bored because the task is too easy or too meaningless?
Is the task too hard so that he is frustrated?

Through this process of design, observation and revision, I can then design the task with the appropriate level of difficulty for him.

'Why do I like Sentosa?'

BACKGROUND

This learning task is a part of Sebastien's 'My Favourite Places' series (see work sample on page 185). With this particular task, I am attempting to expose him to the abstract concepts of the 'why' question and the 'because' response by connecting them to one of his favourite places—Sentosa.

At this juncture, Sebastien has already visited Sentosa several times. So he has already shown his preferences and love for specific places and activities on the island. Not only does he know the names of the different places, he also has specific experiences of these places in his memory bank to make the learning task meaningful for him.

MATERIALS/PREPARATIONS

During our visits to Sentosa, I collected a few different brochures, specifically those that feature his favourite places.

PROCEDURE

1. I introduced Sebastien to the task by talking to him about Sentosa, while showing the brochures that contain photos of his favourite places. During this introduction, I elicited simple 'yes' responses from him by pointing to the places and describing what he liked about the place or the specific activity to ensure that he is even listening to me.

2. Next, I drew lines around the pictures to demarcate the ones that should be cut out for this learning task. Sebastien has come to expect these lines of demarcation to help him to perform his cutting task.

3. Once he finished cutting out the pictures and pasting them on nice coloured papers, I brought out the text I had prepared earlier, which matched each of these pictures. Each of these pictures was accompanied by no more than two or three

sentences of text. He is familiar with most of the words in the sentences.

4. Even though Sebastien still does not speak sentences spontaneously, he has demonstrated an ability to sequence words in a sentence in the written form. Therefore, I am continuously exposing him to sentences so that he will become increasingly comfortable with them. Furthermore, since the sentences are matched with pictures, he is still able to grasp their meaning, which is important in ensuring that he is interested in the learning task.

5. It is also important to highlight the fact that I did not offer him the complete text. Rather, I omitted letters at the end of each word in the text, which needed to be filled in by him. To complete this task, Sebastien was challenged to tap into his memory bank to decide which letters should be inserted and attempt to spell individual words.

6. For example, the text 'Why do I like Sentosa?' becomes:

7. Wh_ d_ I li__ Sent___?

8. When he needed help with the word, I prompted him by sounding out the word phonetically so that he still had to determine the right letters based on the sounds.

9. After filling up the blanks, Sebastien was asked to type the text on the computer. The typing process exposed him to the complete sentences once again. The repetition of the writing task gave him another opportunity to process the language. As mentioned in this book, autistic children, particularly those with language problems, often require repetition to allow them to process all the spoken or written words. Just as significantly, Sebastien was able to experience the language without doing the writing task again. The typing of the words was a new learning experience for him. As far as he was concerned, he was not 'repeating' the task, but doing something different. Obviously, he also practiced using the mouse and the keyboard.

10. Once the text was printed out, I drew lines around each of the sentences. Sebastien then cut out each of the individual sentence strips, which were then pasted on the relevant pages containing the different pictures.
11. For the final step of this learning programme, we read our 'homemade' book in front of the mirror in order to help Sebastien to practise his reading and enunciation skills.

VARIATION - Window Painting Task: 'The Lighthouse and the Whale' (see work sample on page 186)

In this learning task, a fun arts and crafts activity is used as a visual aid to teach Sebastien language. It is important to point out that this arts and crafts task is helpful in getting Sebastien to practise and hone his fine motor control.

To perform this task, Sebastien needs to exert just the right amount of force to squeeze out the paint from the tubes of paint and spread the paint within the contours of the picture (marked by the black lines). Doing this activity also introduces Sebastien to the two different actions of 'squeezing' (the paint out of the tube) and 'spreading' (the paint throughout the picture). It was quite messy in the beginning, but he finally distinguished between the two instructions with repeated verbal prompting and hand-over-hand assistance.

While the above description might have made the task seem arduous, I want to highlight the fact that this task has tremendous appeal to Sebastien for several reasons. First of all, he is inherently drawn to this task because he is obsessed with colours. Furthermore, he is fascinated by the transformation of the paint into a sticky texture that can be peeled off the plastic and pasted onto another surface.

Once the arts and crafts part is completed, I introduce the language portion by posing the basic question: 'What is in this picture?' As with the Sentosa task, I offer the text with incomplete words and Sebastien has to fill in the blanks and type it on the laptop.

Sentosa

Why do I like Sentosa?

Because I like to ride on the Sky Tower, swim and play at the beach.

Mathematics

BACKGROUND

For some autistic children such as Sebastien, mathematics, with its utilisation of abstract symbols (numbers and addition/subtraction signs), can be a particularly meaningless and daunting subject. In order to overcome Sebastien's difficulties with abstractions, I figured out that I needed to forge associations between the mathematical symbols and operations and actual objects. Therefore, the use of counters or any objects for counting was effective for introducing Sebastien to numbers with their visual correspondences.

Furthermore, because Sebastien preferred contextualised learning to decontextualised learning, I introduced problem-based sums to him fairly early in the process to increase the meaningfulness of the addition and subtraction tasks. Instead of simply dealing with numbers and addition or subtraction signs, Sebastien could work with visual images or actual objects.

PROCEDURE

1. In this 'trees' math problem (please refer to the work sample on page 189), Sebastien was expected to read each sentence and convert them into images. As you can see, I provided the boxes and the pictures of the table as prompts for Sebastien to draw the specific number of trees. This visual conversion of the words into images also tested his understanding of the meaning of the sentences. Thus, even a mathematical problem can also be used to help Sebastien to practise his language skills.

2. Moreover, the drawing of the trees was a relatively new challenge for Sebastien who lacked the confidence and the fine motor control to execute any type of drawings. Thus, the drawing of the trees also allowed him to work on his fine motor skills. The colouring of the pictures was the 'reward'

activity for Sebastien, which further motivated him to perform the learning task.

3. Sebastien was also asked to fill in the blanks underneath each of the boxes to help him to organise his thought processes during the conversion from the problem sum to the visual images. At the same time, he also practiced writing the words and matching them to the pictures.

4. Finally, he filled in the blanks of the numbers and signs that set out the equation to complete the entire conversion process:

5. **words —› pictures —› mathematical equation**

6. Requiring Sebastien to write down the equation also helped me to assess whether he truly understood the concept of addition in this problem sum by seeing which sign he would insert into the missing box.

VARIATION

Apart from using two-dimensional pictures and images, you can also act out your problem-based sum to make it even more meaningful for your child, if he or she prefers this form of learning. The actual physical activity involved in the 'acting' experience can help to reinforce your child's learning.

Here is an example of a problem sum that can be acted out in a very simple fashion:

Sebastien has 15 markers.
Sebastien gives mama 8 markers.
How many markers does Sebastien have now? _____ markers

1. After reading the first sentence, simply have your child count out 15 markers from his box.

2. When he has read the second sentence, he needs to physically hand over 8 markers to you, while you give him a clue phrase: '8 markers go bye bye' (clue words). The clue phrase 'bye bye' is associated with 'minus'.

3. Then he is prompted to fill in the equation.

There are 6 trees at the beach.

There are 11 trees at the park.

There are 4 trees by the house

How many trees are there altogether? 21 trees

6 trees

beach

4 trees

park

4 trees

house

6 ⊞ 11 ⊞ & 4 = 21

Recommended Books for Further Reading

Gach, Michael Reed. *Acupressure's Potent Points: A Guide to Self-Care for Common Ailments*. New York: Bantam Books, 1990.

Hendricks, Gay, Jr., *Conscious Breathing: Breathwork for Health, Stress Release, and Personal Mastery*. New York: Bantam Books, 1995.

Grandin, Temple. *Emergence: Labeled Autistic*. Novato: Arena Press, 1986.

Grandin, Temple. *Thinking in Pictures: And Other Reports from My Life with Autism*. New York, Vintage Books, 1996.

Greenspan, Stanley I., and Serena Wieder. *The Child with Special Needs: Encouraging Intellectual and Emotional Growth*. Reading: Perseus Books, 1998.

Gutstein, Steven E. and Rachelle K. Sheely. *Relationship Development Intervention with Children, Adolescents and Adults: Social and Emotional Development Activities for Asperger Syndrome, Autism, PDD and NLD*. London and Philadelphia: Jessica Kingsley Publishers, 2002.

Kranowitz, Carol Stock. *The Out-of-Sync Child: Recognizing and Coping with Sensory Integration Dysfunction*. New York: Penguin Putnam, 2001.

Maurice, Catherine. *Let Me Hear Your Voice: A Family's Triumph Over Autism*. New York: Fawcett Columbine, 1993.

Quill, Karen Ann. *Teaching Children with Autism: Strategies to Enhance Communication and Socialization*. Albany: Delmar Publishers, 1995.

Acknowledgements

This book is a culmination of my journey of raising Sebastien—one that has been accompanied by heartaches, anxieties, mistakes, growing strength and wonder moments. I would not have survived this journey and lived to tell the tale, if not for the following people:

To begin with, I would like to thank various representatives of Marshall Cavendish International for taking a leap of faith in me by publishing this work: Elsa Tan, Violet Phoon, Rizza Manaois and Aria Ting.

I would like to salute the handful of caring professionals and educators in the fields of special education who have given me considerable guidance and support, especially during the early days: Audra, Stacey, Lisa, Perla, Karin and Matt.

Much love and appreciation also go to my old and more recent friends who have gone above and beyond to embrace us with their love and compassion: Jessica, Lisa, Louis and Joyce, Joyce L., Roger and Jan, Marcio, Yong Chien and Lay Leng.

Many thanks also go out to Rachel who saw my need for ongoing support and sustenance by introducing me to an incredible church cell group whose members have inspired and touched me with their open spirits, spiritual strength and kindness: Siew Hoon and Jon, Bee Leng, Cindy and Jeremy, Irene and Kenneth, Chin Cheng and Kenneth, and others who I consider to be a part of my extended family of choice.

I would also like to express my gratitude to my family particularly my mother and relatives who have rallied around me and supported me in various aspects of my life.

Last, but not least, I would like to thank Yuri, my husband, who has propped me up throughout most of this journey, by offering his unique perspectives and making me laugh during the difficult times.

About the Author

Choo Kah Ying is a writer/educator who is currently homeschooling her ten-year-old autistic son. Since her return to Singapore in 2005, after living and working as an academic researcher in the US for more than a decade, Ms Choo has been active in raising public awareness about autism and empowering parents of autistic children. She published articles on raising and educating autistic children in *The Straits Times* and *Today*. Apart from writing articles and publishing a picture book on her son, she also offers parent training programmes, individualised consultations and other support services. She lives in Singapore with her husband and son. (For more information about the author, please go to http://autismworld.blogspot.com.)